TEN YEARS' DIGGING

IN EGYPT

1881—1891

W. M. FLINDERS PETRIE

AUTHOR OF 'PYRAMIDS OF GIZEH,' 'HAWARA,' 'MEDUM,' ETC.

WITH A MAP

AND ONE HUNDRED AND SIXTEEN ILLUSTRATIONS

ISBN: 978-1-63923-987-0

Printed: March 2023

Published and Distributed By:
Lushena Books
607 Country Club Drive, Unit E
Bensenville, IL 60106
www.lushenabks.com

ISBN: 978-1-63923-987-0

PORTRAITS PAINTED IN WAX, FROM ROMAN MUMMIES, HAWARA.

See page 97.

'IN STUDYING HISTORY, IT MUST BE BORNE IN MIND THAT A KNOWLEDGE IS NECESSARY OF THE STATE OF MANNERS, CUSTOMS, WEALTH, ARTS, AND SCIENCE AT THE DIFFERENT PERIODS TREATED OF. THE TEXT OF CIVIL HISTORY REQUIRES A CONTEXT OF THIS KNOWLEDGE IN THE MIND OF THE READER.'

Sir Arthur Helps on History.

PREFACE

ALTHOUGH the discoveries which are related in this volume have been already published, yet there is to be considered the large number of readers who feed in the intermediate regions between the arid highlands and mountain ascents of scientific memoirs, and the lush—not to say rank—marsh-meadows of the novel and literature of amusement.

Those, then, who wish to grasp the substance of the results, without the precision of the details, are the public for whom this is written ; and I trust that, out of consideration for their feelings, hardly a single measurement or rigid statement can be found here from cover to cover. Any one who wants detail can find it in the various annual volumes which have already appeared. Several of the finest objects found appear here, however, for the first time in illustration ; for having been kept in Egypt I only had photographs to work from, which were, as yet, unused.

The work described here is not by any means all that 'has occupied my time in these years ; much exploring has also been done, and dozens of ancient towns have been visited, and their remains examined ; but such work is rather a basis for further results than a source of interest in itself to the public. Besides this I have been occupied in Palestine.

I may as well remark that the first two years' work were done entirely as a private matter ; though the Royal Society afterwards made a grant to cover the greater part of the cost of its publication. The three following years' work was carried on for the Egypt Exploration Fund ; but as the management of that society was not what I had expected, I preferred to withdraw, without personal unpleasantness; in fact, some promoters of it have been more my friends since then than they were before. For a year I rather explored than excavated, having indeed no prospect of funds at my disposal for the purpose. But to my surprise, two supporters of the subject appeared independently, Mr. Jesse Haworth, and then Mr. Martyn Kennard ; all expenses of excavation and transport in the last four years' work, have been at their charge ; and the objects found, and not kept for the Egyptian Museum, or retained for private friends, have been presented by them to various public collections. Thus three years have been private work, three years with the Fund, and four years with other friends.

One of the pleasantest results of my work has been the number of co-operators who have appeared, and the friendships that have resulted. In fact an informal body of workers have come together, all attracted by a real love of work, and not by publicity or the buttering and log-rolling of societies. Without any parade of empty names, or speechifying, we each know where to turn for co-operation, and how to join hands to help in the work.

To many the interest of these researches will be the solidity and reality which they give to what we only knew as yet on paper. When we read of 'Pharaoh's house in Tahpanhes,' and then see Defennch explaining the narrative,—when Ezekiel wrote of Javan being 'merchants,' and 'going to and fro, occupied in the fairs' of Tyre, and we see the widespread trade of the Ionians as early as Gurob,—when we read in Homer of the prehistoric civilization, and see the actual products of those races brought to light,—we feel how real was the life of which the outlines have come down to us across the ages.

I hope that among my readers there may be some who are not of the superficial class, for whom the tender-foot directions of guide-books are written, and the luxuries of hotels are provided as attractions; so I have given some hints as to how a traveller may go about in Egypt without the usual routine of coddling, and being led by the nose by a dragoman. If the active tripper is thereby induced to take an active trip in Egypt, and—contrary to the custom of most tourists—subordinate the stomach to the intellect, I shall be very glad to make his acquaintance there.

CONTENTS

LIST OF ILLUSTRATIONS

KINGS AND DYNASTIES NAMED IN THIS VOLUME

(The last terms are used vaguely for general indications.)

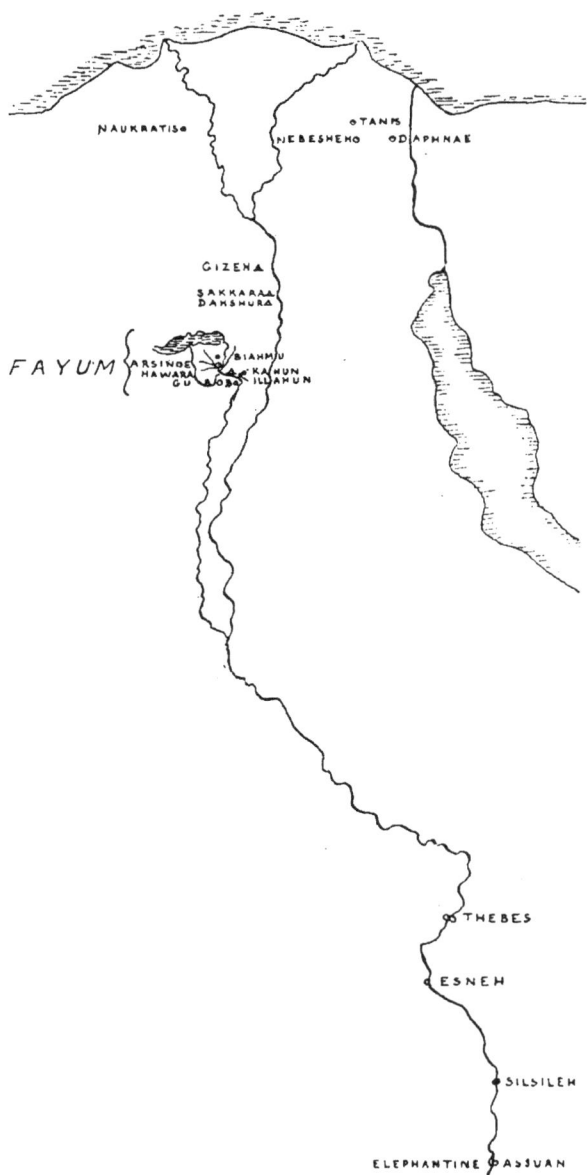

NAUKRATIS•

○TANIS
NEBESHEH○   ○D|APHNAE

GIZEH▲

SAKKARA▲▲▲
DAHSHUR▲

FAYUM } ARSINOE•
HAWARA•   •|BIAHMU
GU•▲○B○ KAHUN
              ILLAHUN

○○THEBES

•ESNEH

•SILSILEH

ELEPHANTINE •ASSUAN

POSITION OF PLACES IN EGYPT NAMED IN THIS VOLUME.

1. THE PYRAMIDS OF GIZEH.

CHAPTER I.

THE PYRAMIDS OF GIZEH.

1881–2.

WHEN, in the end of 1880, I first started for Egypt, I had long been preparing for the expedition ; during a couple of years before that measuring instruments, theodolites, rope-ladders, and all the *impedimenta* for scientific work, had been prepared and tested. To start work under circumstances so different to those of any European country, and where many customary appliances were not to be obtained, required necessarily much prearrangement and consideration ; though on the whole my subsequent experience has been that of decreasing the baggage, and simplifying one's requirements.

The first consideration on reaching Egypt was where to be housed. In those days there was no luxurious hotel close to the pyramids ; if any one

needed to live there, they must either live in a tomb
or in the Arab village.   As an English engineer had
left a tomb fitted with door and shutters I was glad
to get such accommodation.   When I say a tomb, it
must be understood to be the upper chamber where
the Egyptian fed his ancestors with offerings, not the
actual sepulchre.   And I had three rooms, which had

2. MY TOMB AT GIZEH.

belonged to separate tombs originally; the thin walls
of rock which the economical Egyptian left between
his cuttings, had been broken away, and so I had a
doorway in the middle into my living-room, a window
on one side for my bedroom, and another window
opposite for a store-room.   I resided here for a great
part of two years; and often when in draughty houses,
or chilly tents, I have wished myself back in my tomb.
No place is so equable in heat and cold, as a room
cut out in solid rock; it seems as good as a fire in
cold weather, and deliciously cool in the heat.

I lived then, as I have since in Egypt, independent
of servants.   The facilities of preserved provisions, and

the convenience of petroleum stoves, enable one to do without the annoyance of having some one about meddling with everything. I had one of the most intelligent men of the place, Ali Gabri, to help me with the work, and his nephew and slave used to sleep in the next tomb (on the right of the sketch) as my guards at night. Such was my first taste of sweet independence from civilization.

The object in view for which the work was undertaken was to decisively test the various theories concerning the pyramids, which were then being widely discussed on very insufficient knowledge. If all, or any, of these theories were correct, there were some very tough questions to be picked over between different parties; but the first question to be settled was whether the theories agreed with the actual facts of the case, as if they did not there was no need of further discussion. They must pass the test of fact before they could be further considered on the grounds of their abstract probability or metaphysical coherence. One of the most obvious of all the facts, and most deeply concerned in the various theories, was the actual size of the great pyramid ; yet this was not known with any accuracy, the best measurements varying by several feet. Most of the theories involved the notion of extreme accuracy of workmanship, yet we were entirely ignorant of the amount of accuracy in the form of the pyramid, and in most of its internal construction.

It may not be amiss here to point out what is the meaning of accuracy. One often hears that something is 'quite accurate.' If I ask a workman if his work is accurate, he will indignantly refer to his foot-rule to prove it; but if you were to ask if his foot-rule is accurate he would doubt your sanity. What is accuracy for one purpose is inaccuracy for another. Children build castles on the sand, and make them perhaps tidy enough; but their accuracy would not do for laying out a garden; nor would the garden bed quite do to regulate the straightness of a tennis court. When a house is planned, still further particularity is needed for the accuracy of its squareness and straightness; and yet the joiner needs a better straight edge than the bricklayer. In turn the joiner's ideas would never suffice for the accuracy of putting together a Forth bridge, with its lengths of furlongs of steel, needed to exactly fit into place. And even beyond that, the telescope maker, dividing his circles, or polishing his object glasses, must attend to quantities which are quite beyond the accuracies of the engineer. There are as many kinds of accuracy as there are of cleanliness, from the cleanness of a clean-swept path, up to the absolute lifelessness and chemical purity of some tedious preparation in the laboratory.

There is, therefore, no such thing as absolute accuracy; what is called accuracy in each business is that amount of inaccuracy which is insignificant. If we want to understand what kind of precision the ancients aimed at, our errors in examining their work must be so small as to be insignificant by the side of their errors. If they went to the nearest hundredth of an inch, we must go to the nearest thousandth, in order to know what their ideas of accuracy were.

The main work of the first season, therefore, con-

sisted in making a very precise triangulation all over
the hill of Gizeh ; including points around all the
three pyramids, and on the temples and walls belonging to them.   A fine theodolite was used, by which
single seconds of angle could be read ; and the obser-

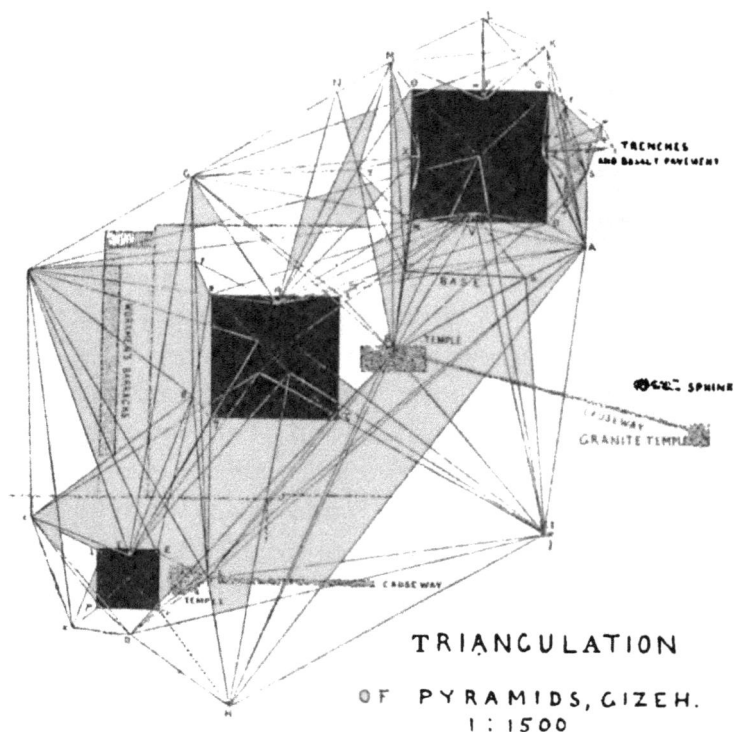

TRIANGULATION
OF PYRAMIDS, GIZEH.
1 : 1500

vations were repeated so many times, that if I finished
the work at a single station in one day I was well satis-
fied.   The result of all this mass of checked observa-
tions, after duly reducing and computing, was that there
was scarcely a point about which one quarter inch of
uncertainty remained, and most of the points were
fixed to within one-tenth of an inch.   These points

were, however, only arbitrary marks put on suitable spots of the rock ; and it needed a good deal of less elaborate work to connect these with the traces of the ancient constructions near them. The second season I obtained permission from Prof. Maspero to search for the ancient casing and points of construction of the pyramids. Many points were found easily enough ; but some required long and dangerous work. To reach the casing, which still remains at the middle of each side of the great pyramid, was a hard matter ; it was heaped over with broken chips a dozen to twenty feet deep, and they lay so loosely that they soon fell into any hole that we dug. It was needful therefore to begin with a very wide space, and gradually taper the hole, walling the sides roughly with loose blocks. Thus we succeeded in finding the casing on each of the three sides, where it was as yet unknown ; the north casing having been cleared by a huge excavation of Col. Vyze over forty years before. These holes were very ticklish places, make them as we would ; the Arabs dared not work them, and I had to get negroes to face the business. As it was, we could not venture to knock a bit of the stone, for fear of the vibration loosening the sides ; and I was all but buried once, when—just as I had come out of the bottom of the hole—many tons of stones went pouring down the pit from the loose stuff above.

At the third pyramid the difficulty was varied ; there the pyramid was encumbered with loose blocks lying on a bed of sand. So soon then as we dug into the sand, the blocks came sliding down into our hole. But here the matter was settled by adding more stones, and so wedging all the blocks around into a ring ; thus they balanced around the hole, and kept each other out.

The casing of the third pyramid has never been finished.

The outer sides of the granite blocks were left with an excess of stone, in order to protect them in transport from Assuan, and this was never removed by dressing

4. GRANITE CASING THIRD PYRAMID.

down, as had been intended. Thus in some examples —as above—the stone sticks out far beyond where the face was to be. In the granite temple the same method was followed, but there the wall was dressed, and hence each stone at the corners of the chambers turns a little way round the adjacent walls, so that the corner is cut out of solid stone all the way up.

The temple of the third pyramid is the most complete, and gives the best notion of the enclosures around the cell or chamber, in which the offerings to the deceased king were presented.   This view is from the top of the pyramid, looking down into it. At the end of its causeway are a few trees, and a hill on the right, with remains of another causeway leading from it to the plain.

5. TEMPLE OF THIRD PYRAMID.

Of the inside of the pyramids there were already numerous measurements recorded, which showed that small differences and errors existed in ·the work ; but some fresh and more accurate methods of examination were needed.   Instead then of simply measuring from wall to wall, and remaining in ignorance of where the discrepancies lay, I always used plumb-lines for measuring all upright faces, and a levelling instrument for all horizontal surfaces. By hanging a plumb-line in each corner of a room, and measuring from it to the walls at many parts of the height, and then observing the distances of the plumb-lines on the floor, it is easy to find the dimensions of the room at any level, and to know exactly where the faults of construction lie. The same principle gives us the readiest way of examining a solid, such as a sarcophagus; and we can thus, in a few hours, do more than in as many days' work with elaborate apparatus. Some thread, and a piece of wax to stick it on with, are all that is needed beside the plain measuring rods.

The results of thus attacking the subject were, that on the one hand most brilliant workmanship was disclosed, while on the other hand it was intermingled with some astonishing carelessness and clumsiness. The laying out of the base of the great pyramid of Khufu is a triumph of skill; its errors, both in length and in angles, could be covered by placing one's thumb on them ; and to lay out a square of more than a furlong in the side (and with rock in the midst of it, which prevented any diagonal checks being measured) with such accuracy shows surprising care. The work of the casing stones which remain is of the same class; the faces are so straight and so truly square, that when the stones were built together the film of mortar left between them is on an average not thicker than one's thumb nail, though the joint is a couple of yards long ; and the levelling of them over long distances has not any larger errors.   In the inside of the pyramid the same fine work is seen : the entrance passage joints are in many cases barely visible when searched for; in the Queen's chamber, when the encrusting salt is scraped away, the joints are found with cement not thicker than a sheet of paper ; while in the King's chamber the granite courses have been dressed to a fine equality, not

6. CASING BENEATH RUBBISH NORTH OF PYRAMID.
ARAB HOLE ABOVE IT.

varying more than a straw's breadth in a furlong length of blocks.

Side by side with this splendid work are the strangest mistakes.   After having levelled the casing so finely, the builders made a hundred times the error in levelling the shorter length of the King's chamber, so that they might have done it far better by just looking at the horizon.   After having dressed the casing joints so beautifully, they left the face of the wall in the grand gallery rough chiselled. The design was changed, and a rough shaft was cut from the side of the gallery, down through the building and the rock, to the lower end of the entrance passage. The granite in the ante-chamber is left without its final dressing. And the kernel of the whole, the sarcophagus, has much worse work in it than in the building, or than in other sarcophagi of the same period. The meaning of this curious discrepancy seems to be that the original architect, a true master of accuracy and fine methods, must have ceased to superintend the work when it was but half done. His personal influence gone, the training of his school was not sufficient to carry out the remainder of the building in the first style. Thus the base and the casing around it, the building of the Queen's chamber, and the preparation of the granite for the King's chamber, must all have had the master's eye ; but the carelessness of the pupils appears so soon as the control was removed. Mere haste will not account for egregious mistakes, such as that of the King's chamber level, which the skilful architect would have remedied by five minutes' observation. This suggests that the exquisite workmanship often found in the early periods, did not so much depend on a large school or wide-spread ability, as on a few men far above their fellows, whose every touch was a triumph. In this way we can reconcile it with the crude, and often clumsy, work in building and sculpture found in the same ages. There were no trades union rules against 'besting one's mates' in those days, any more than in any business at present where real excellence is wanted.

The results were decidedly destructive for the theories. The fundamental length of the base of the pyramid does not agree to any of the theoretical needs : and though no doubt some comfort has been extracted from hypothetical lengths of what the pyramid base would be if continued down to levels below the pavement (such as the different sockets), yet no such bases ever existed, nor could even be guessed at or theorised on, so long as the pyramid base was intact, as the sockets were entirely covered by casing and pavement. Various other theories fare as badly ; and the only important one which is well established is that the angle of the outside was such as to make the base circuit equal to a circle struck by the height as a radius. See also the account of Medum.

The second pyramid was built by Khafra. His name was first found with it on the piece of a mace-head of white stone, which I found in the temple. The form is here completed from another head of the twelfth dynasty ; and drawings of maces from Medum show the head and stick entire. In accuracy Khafra's work is inferior to that of Khufu. The errors of the pyramid length are double, and of angle quadruple that found in the earlier work, and the bulk of its masonry is far rougher. But the sarcophagus in it is of much better work, without any mistakes, and generally showing more experience and ability. The third pyramid, of Menkaura, is again inferior to the second, in both its outer form and internal work. It has moreover been most curiously altered ; originally intended to be of small size, it has been greatly enlarged, not by repeated coatings, but at one

operation. The original entrance passage was aban-
doued, and the chamber was deepened, another passage
cut from the inside outwards so as to emerge lower

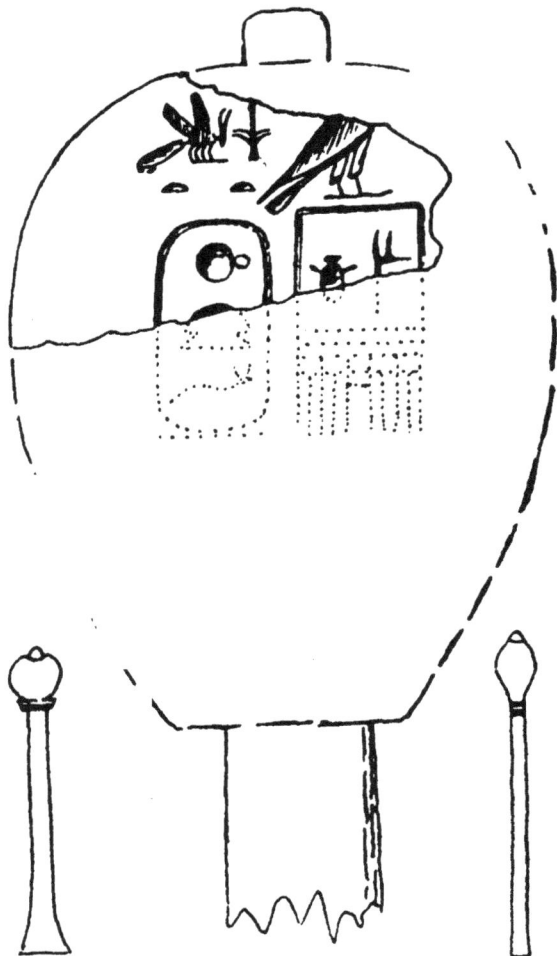

7. MACE-HEAD OF KHAPRA.

down, and another chamber excavated below the level
of the first, and lined with granite.

Some very usual fallacies with regard to the

pyramids were also disposed of.   The passages are
commonly supposed to have been blocked up by

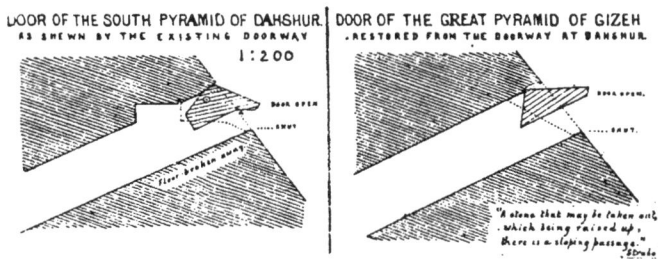

DOOR OF THE SOUTH PYRAMID OF DAHSHUR. | DOOR OF THE GREAT PYRAMID OF GIZEH
AS SHEWN BY THE EXISTING DOORWAY | RESTORED FROM THE DOORWAY AT DAHSHUR.
1 : 200

8. PYRAMID DOORS.

plugs of stone ; whereas in both the great and second
pyramids there is proof in the passages that no such

9. PIVOT HOLE OF DOOR AND CUTTING OF ROOF ;
SOUTH PYRAMID, DAHSHUR.

blocks ever existed.   The entrances are supposed to
have been concealed by the solid masonry ; whereas
at Dahshur, and in Strabo's account of the great

pyramid, it is evident that a flap-door of stone filled the passage mouth, and allowed of its being passed. The pyramids are supposed to have been built by continuous additions during a king's life, and ended only by his death ; whereas there is no evidence of this in any of them, and it is clearly disproved by the construction and arrangement of the interiors; the plan was entire originally, and the whole structure begun at once. The sarcophagi are often supposed to have been put in to the pyramids at the king's burial, with his body inside ; whereas in the great and second pyramids they will not pass through the passages. and must have been built in. The casing is supposed to have been all built in the rough, and cut to its slope afterwards ; whereas the remaining blocks at the base slightly differ in angle side by side, proving that they were dressed before building in.

Besides examining the pyramids, the remains of the temple of the great pyramid were cleared, and the granite temple of Khafra was thoroughly measured and planned. But perhaps the most interesting part of the subject was tracing how the work was done. The great barracks of the workmen were found, behind the second pyramid, capable of housing four thousand men; and such was probably the size of the trained staff of skilled masons employed on the pyramid building. Besides these a large body of mere labourers were needed to move the stones ; and this was probably done during the inundation, when water carriage is easier, and the people have no work. Herodotos gives the echo of this, when he says that the relays of labourers only worked for three months at a time. It would be quite prae-

ticable to build the great pyramid in the time, and
with the staff of labourers assigned by Herodotos.

Tools are needed as well as labour ; and the question
of what tools were used is now settled by evidence, to
which modern engineers cordially agree.   I found

10. SAWN BASALT.

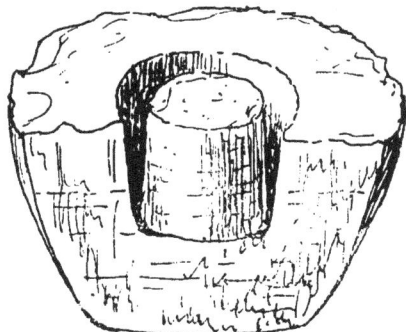

12. GRANITE DRILL CORE.

11. TUBULAR DRILL HOLE.

repeatedly that the hard stones, basalt, granite, and
diorite, were sawn ; and that the saw was not a blade,
or wire, used with a hard powder, but was set with
fixed cutting points, in fact, a jewelled saw.   These
saws must have been as much as nine feet in length,
as the cuts run lengthwise on the sarcophagi.   One of

the most usual tools was the tubular drill, and this was also set with fixed cutting points ; I have a core from inside a drill hole, broken away in the working, which shows the spiral grooves produced by the cutting points as they sunk down into the material ; this is of red granite, and there has been no flinching or jumping of the tool ;

13. GRAVING IN DIORITE.

every crystal, quartz, or felspar, has been cut through in the most equable way, with a clean irresistible cut. An engineer, who knows such work with diamond drills as well as any one, said to me, ' I should be proud to turn out such a finely cut core now : ' and truth to tell, modern drill cores cannot hold a candle to the Egyptians : by the side of the ancient work they look wretchedly scraped out and irregular. That such hard cutting points were known and used is proved by clean cut fine hieroglyphs on dio-

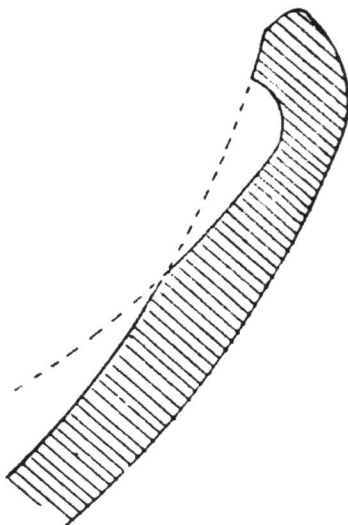

14. SECTION OF BOWL TURNED WITH RADIUS TOOL.

rite, engraved without a trace of scraping ; and by the lathe work, of which I found pieces of turned bowls with the tool lines on them, and positive proof that the surface had not been ground out. The lathe tools were fixed as in modern times, to sweep regular arcs from a centre; and the work is fearless and powerful, as in a flat diorite table with foot, turned in one piece; and also surpassingly delicate, as in a bowl of diorite, which around the body is only as thick as stout card. The great granite sarcophagi were sawn outside, and hollowed by cutting rows of tube drill holes, as may be seen in the great pyramid. No doubt much hammer - dressing was also used, as in all periods; but the fine work shows the marks of just such tools as we have only now re-invented. We can thus understand, far more than before, how the marvellous works of the Egyptians were executed; and further insight only shows plainer the true skill and ability of which they were masters in the earliest times that we can trace.

15. PLUMMET OF KHUFU.   1 : 2.

16. GIZEH PYRAMIDS FROM THE DESERT.

17. TEMPLE OF TANIS FROM EAST END; PYLON IN DISTANCE.

CHAPTER II.

TANIS.

1884.

AFTER a year in England, for the working out and publication of the survey at the pyramids, described in the last chapter, I undertook to excavate for the Egypt Exploration Fund. And as great things were then expected from Tanis, and a special fund of £1000 was in course of being raised for its clearance, the most desirable course was to ascertain what prospects really existed there. A preliminary exploring trip was made to several places in the Delta, in course of which I discovered Naukratis ; and as soon as the marshes had somewhat dried I went in February to Tanis. It is an out-of-the-way place, inaccessible except by water during some months, twenty miles from a post or station ; on three sides the marshy plains stretch away to the horizon, only a little cultivation existing on the south. When I arrived the mounds were almost impassable for the mud, and continual storms threatened my tent. But gradually I built a house on the top of the mounds, and from thence looked down over the work on one side, and over the village on the other.

Tanis is a great ring of mounds, around the wide plain in which lie the temple ruins. And the first day I went over it I saw that the temple site was worked out ; the limits of the ruins had been reached, and no more statues or buildings should be hoped for, by the side of what was already known. But such were the large expectations about the site, that I had to prove the case, by a great amount of fruitless trenching in all directions. The only monuments that we unearthed were far out of the temple, in a Ptolemaic shrine ; this contained a fine stele of Ptolemy II and Arsinoe, which was entirely gilt when discovered, and two or three other steles, the recess containing the large stele being flanked by two sphinxes. The main stele and sphinxes are now in the British Museum.

But though digging was not productive in the temple, yet I found two important monuments which had been exposed by Mariette's excavators, and yet were never noticed by himself, De Rougé, or others who studied the remains. One was a part of an obelisk of the thirteenth dynasty, with an inscription of a king's son, Nchesi, perhaps the son of the king Nchesi-Ra. The other was the upper part of the well-known stele of Tirhaka: this I found lying face up ; and on search-

18. STELE OF PTOLEMY II.

ing every block of the same quality for the remainder of it, I turned up the lower half, which Mariette had hidden ; thus the unknown led me to the known.

There was, however, plenty of work to do in examining thoroughly, and planning, all the remains, which—

as we have just noticed—were but scantily attended to before. The fallen blocks of the granite pylon needed to be turned over, as they were all cut out of older sculptures; and to do this without tackle, I dug a trench on one side of the heap of blocks, and then rolled them over one by one into it, so as to turn them. In this way I examined every block, and discovered the fragments of the enormous colossus of Ramessu II in red granite, which must have been about 80 feet high, and have towered far above the temple roofs, amid the forest of obelisks which adorned the city. The toe alone is as large as a man's body. Some large statues were also found by the road leading up to the temple. And every block of the hundreds which strew the ground here was examined on all sides, by mining beneath it where needful; every fragment of inscription was copied; and finally a plan was made, showing the place of each block, with numbers affixed referring to the inscriptions. Thus anyone can draw their own conelusions as to the arrangement of the place, and the positions of the monuments, better in their arm-chair than by wandering over the chaos of dilapidation in the plain of Zoan.

Finding that no great discoveries could reward me in the temple, I tried the outskirts of the town, but only found a very late cemetery of no importance. I tried also sinking pits, in hopes of reaching the early town of the Ramessides or the Hyksos; but in vain, as the accumulation of Greek and Roman remains blocked the way, after descending even thirty feet. Then the houses of the Roman period on the surface were examined. One yielded a jar in the corner of the cellar, in which the lady had hidden away a large silver chain, a necklace of fine stones, and a gold ring.

But the burnt houses were the real prize of the season, as the owners had fled and left most of their goods ; and the reddened patches of earth attracted us usually to a profitable site. In one house there was a beautiful marble term, of Italian work ; and the fragments of a very curious zodiac,

19. GOLD RING. 1 : 1.

painted on a sheet of clear glass over a foot square, each sign or month having an emblematic head to represent it ; unhappily, it was broken in a hundred and fifty pieces, and as I uncovered them it was cruel to see the gold foil work which was on them peel off on to the earth. leaving the glass bare in many parts. A yet more heartrending sight was the pile of papyrus rolls, so rotted that they fell to pieces with a touch, showing here and there a letter of the finest Greek writing. The next house, also burnt, was the best of all. Here we found the limestone statuette of the owner, Baka-khuiu, inscribed in demotic on the base ; a sensible, sturdy-looking, active man, who seems to have been a lawyer or notary, to judge by his documents. Many household objects of pottery and stone were found, jars, mortars, &c., and a beautiful blue-glazed jar, perhaps the largest such known, and quite perfect. The rich result, however, was in his waste ; for in a recess under the cellar stairs had been five baskets of

D

20. BAKAKHUIU.

old papyri. Though many had utterly perished by being burnt to white ash, yet one basketful was only carbonized; and tenderly undermining the precious black mass, I shifted it out and carried it up to my house with fear and reverent joy. It took ten hours' work to separate safely all the documents, twisted, crushed, and squeezed together, and all as brittle as only burnt papyrus is; a bend, or a jerk, and the piece was ruined. At last, I had over a hundred and fifty documents separated; and, each wrapped apart, and put in tin boxes, they travelled safely. They have now all been opened, and glazed; and two of them already prove to be of the greatest interest. One is a book of hieroglyphic signs in columns, followed by their hieratic equivalents, and the school-name by which they were learned: the greater part of this is preserved, and shows us, for the first time, the system on which the hieroglyphics were arranged and taught.

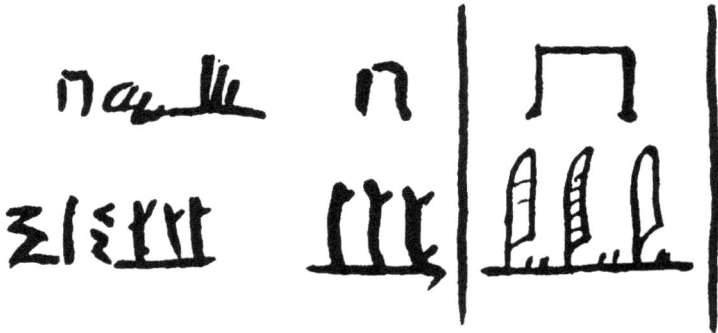

The other is a geographical papyrus, forestalling Brugsch's great work on the geography and the nome divisions of Egypt ; though defective in part all through, it is of the greatest value.   Most of the other papyri are in demotic, and still await reading, while some are in Greek.   Of course, being carbonized, the whole mass is black, and it is only by reflected light that it is possible to read anything ; when the illumination is properly arranged, the duller surface of the ink can be seen on the brighter face of the papyrus.   It is seldom such a treasure as this basketful of knowledge is so narrowly saved from destruction ; a little more air in the burning, a little less care in the unearthing, the separation, the packing, or the opening, and these documents would have disappeared. Of course, under the usual system of leaving Arab overseers to manage excavations, all such discoveries are utterly destroyed.

CHAPTER III.

NAUKRATIS.

1885.

BEFORE beginning work in the end of 1883 I visited Gizeh ; and, as usual, many small antiquities were offered to me by the Arabs. Among such was the upper part of an alabaster figure of a soldier, wearing a helmet and armlets, which was plainly of archaic Greek or Cypriote work. I at once gave the man what he asked for it (never run risks in important cases), and then enquired where he got it. ' From Nebireh,' was his answer, and that was somewhere near Damanhur. So, a month or two later, I took an opportunity of going down to that region, and, after some mistakes and enquiries, I at last reached the place, in course of a twenty mile walk, and having only half-an-hour to spare before going on to the train. There I met a sight which I had never hoped for,—almost too strange to believe. Before me lay a long low mound of town ruins, of which all the core had been dug out by the natives for earth, thus baring the very lowest level of the town all over the middle of it. Wherever I walked in this crater I trod on pieces of archaic Greek pottery ; soon I laded my pockets with scraps of vases and of statuettes, and at last tore myself away, longing to resolve the mystery

23. CYPRIOTE SOLDIER.

of these Greeks in Egypt. Up to that time no Greek remains earlier than the Ptolemaic age, and Alexander, had been found in the country, and to step back two or three centuries, into the days of black-figured and rosette-ornamented vases, and archaic statuettes, was quite a new departure.

That season's work was already laid out, and I
was bound to go to Tanis ; but the next season I
returned to this curious site, determined to understand
its history. The only place that I could find to live
in about there was an old country house of a pasha ;
and, while looking at it, I noticed two blocks of dark
grey stone by the side of the entrance. Turning
one of them over, I there saw the glorious heading
ΗΠΟΛΙΣΗΝΑΥΚΡΑΤΙ . . . ; a decree of the city of

HΠΟΛΙΣΗΝΑΥΚΡΑΤΙ
ΗΛΙΟΔΩΡΟΝΔΩΡΙΩΝΟΣΦΙΛΟ · · · ·
ΤΟΝΙΕΡΕΑΤΗΣΑΘΗΝΑΣΔΙΑΒΙΟΥ · · · ·
ΣΥΓΓΡΑΦΟΦΥΛΑΚΑΑΡΕΤΗΣΚΑΙ · · · ·
ΕΝΕΚΑΤΗΣΕΙΣΑΥΤΗΝ ·

24. DEDICATION OF STATUE TO HELIODOROS, BY THE
NAUKRATITES. 1 : 6.

Naukratis was before me, and the unknown town
now had a name ; and that a name which had been
sought for often, and far from this place, and which
was one of the objects of Egyptian research to discover and truly assign. All that day ' Naukratis '
rang in my mind, and I sprang over the mounds with
that splendid exultation of a new discovery, long
wished for and well found. In England, some hesitated, and some doubted, but none denied it ; and
after the season's work there was no longer any
question. The next year I continued the excavations

along with Mr. Ernest Gardner, and was soon able to leave the remainder of the clearing in his hands, while I moved on to fresh discoveries, on the east of the country.

The origin of Naukratis was evidently entirely Greek; down on the flat surface of Nile mud, which shows the level of the country when the city was founded, the earliest remains are Greek potsherds. The date of its foundation was certainly before Amasis; and the discovery of the fort of Defenneh (Tahpanhes) the next year explained the origin of this city. When Psamtik I, in 665 B.C,. had wrested the throne of Egypt from the dodecarchy, or local princes (who had assumed authority on the fall of the Ethiopian rule of Tirhaka), he based his power on ' the brazen men from the sea,' the Karian and Ionian mercenaries. But he knew too well the temper of his countrymen to obtrude this strength needlessly; and at the same time he needed special defence from Libya and from Asia. He therefore planted his Greek troops in two great garrisons, one on his Libyan frontier at Naukratis, the other on his Asiatic frontier at Tahpanhes ; at each place founding a large square fort and a walled camp around it.

These Greeks brought with them their national worship; and of the temples mentioned by Herodotos, those of Apollo, Aphrodite, and Hera, have been found, and also one to the Dioskouroi, not recorded in history. The temple of the Milesian Apollo appears to have been the oldest : it stood in the centre of the town, outside of the fort, and was first built of mud-brick, plastered over, and later on—about the fifth century—

of white stone, some pieces of which I found. The
site had been nearly cleared out by the native diggers ;
and I only came in time to get fragments of the
temple, and to open up the great rubbish trench,
where all the temple refuse was thrown. Very pre-

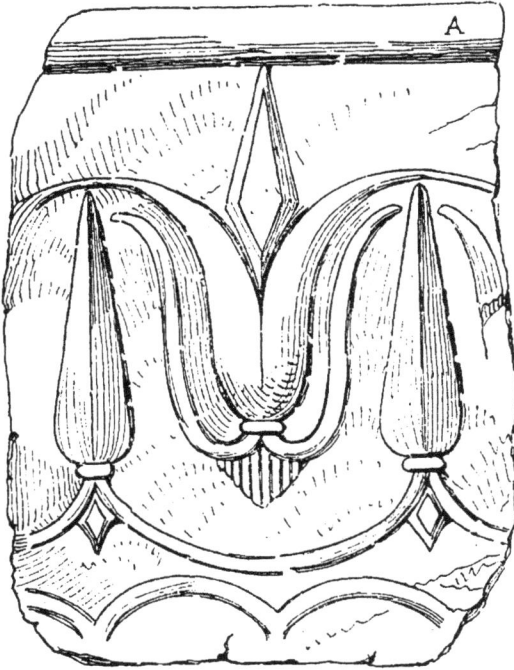

25. NECKING OF COLUMN, APOLLO TEMPLE.

cions this rubbish was to me, layer under layer of
broken vases, from the innumerable small bowls to
the great craters of noble size and design ; and most
precious of all were the hundreds of dedications
inscribed on the pottery, some of them probably the
oldest examples of Greek writing known, and altogether far outnumbering all our past material for the

archaic alphabets. The temple of Aphrodite I found
the next year, and Mr. Gardner cleared it out, and
unearthed three successive buildings, one over the
other. Though, perhaps, as old as that of Apollo, its

26. OLDEST IONIC DEDICATION, 660? B.C.   2 : 5.

inscriptions are not so primitive ; but it has a charm
from the tale of Athenaios about the mariners from
Cyprus, who had a statuette of the goddess a span
high in their boat ; and how they besought it in the
storm, and were soon at peace, and their boat bespread
with myrtle boughs ; wherefore ,they dedicated the

27. NAUKRATITE CUP.   1 : 3.

statuette in the temple of Aphrodite at Naukratis,
and the people of the city made myrtle wreaths for
many an age after. Fine vases were found here ; and
great quantities of a particular kind of cup, which was

apparently made on purpose for offering here. It is a bowl with a very tall upright brim, deeper than the bowl itself, and covered over with a white coat, on which delicate painting in brown is sometimes added; that these were specially made here we know from the name of Aphrodite being painted on one before the baking. The temple of Hera has been entirely swept away, and we only know of its place from some pieces of dedication on bowls found by Mr. Gardner; these lay not far from the Apollo temple, in a great enclosure, which I planned the first

28. EXAMPLES OF DEDICATIONS (TRANSLITERATED) TO APOLLO, APHRODITE, HERA, AND THE DIOSKOUROI. 2 : 3.

season. The Dioskouroi had a small temple near that of Apollo; of which only some brick pillars, and flakes of brilliant red and blue stucco, were found. But several pieces of dedicated bowls showed the nature and early age of this shrine.

The greatest and most celebrated building of Naukratis was the Panhellenion, with the central altar of the Greek community in Egypt. This was in the large enclosure around the fort, as all are agreed; but the depth of earth there prevented my reaching any remains of the altar. Herodotos expressly mentions that certain Greek towns were excluded from the common participation in the Panhellenion, and that hence arose the separate temples in the town. Now as the sanctuary and the fort were in one, it seems readily explained how the mercenaries welcomed their kinsmen and townsfolk in the camp to join at the common altar; while those traders who came from other cities would be left outside, and would found their own temples. If it were so, we may conclude that neither Miletos, Samos, or Aegina, furnished any

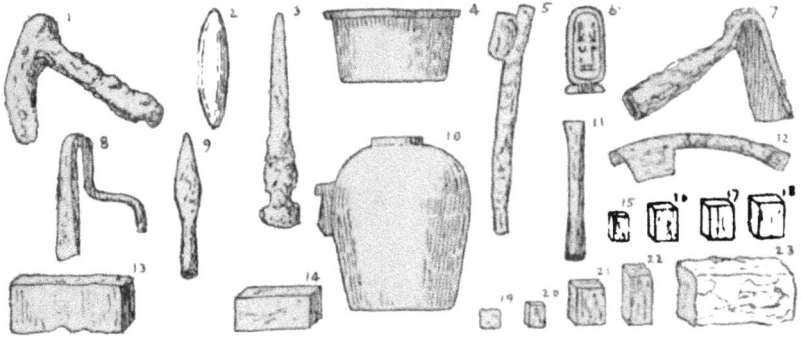

29. FOUNDATION DEPOSIT MODELS. IRON: 1, HOE; 7, MORTAR RAKE. 2, ALABASTER PEG. BRONZE: 3, KNIFE; 5, AXE; 8, ADZE; 9, TROWEL; 11, CHISEL; 12, HATCHET. GLAZED: 4, CUP; 10, LIBATION VASE; 14, BLOCK. 6, NAME OF PTOLEMY II ON LAZULI. MATERIALS: 13, MUD-BRICK; 15–23, TURQUOISE, JASPER, LAZULI, AGATE, GOLD, SILVER, LEAD, COPPER, IRON. 1 : 4.

of the mercenaries of Psamtik. In the time of Ptolemy Philadelphos, as the old camp and Panhellenion no longer needed defence, the entrance was widened and occupied with a large building; of which the foundation deposits, consisting of models of the iron and bronze tools, of the materials, and of the libation vases, were discovered in each corner of the bed of sand which was laid beneath the foundations. An avenue led up to this from the west, and marble rams, a large granite sphinx, and a base of a figure dedi-. cated to Zeus of Thebes (i. e. Amen, identified with Zeus), were found here.

:· To turn now to the town ; probably one of the most important buildings in the fifth century B. C. was the palaistra, dedicated to Apollo by Kleainetos, Aristo-themios, and Maiandrios, according to the beautiful marble inscription found here. Unfortunately we do not know the site of it, as the inscribed block had

30. DEDICATION OF PALAISTRA. 1 : 6.

been re-used in later times, and was also dug up before I went to the place. It was shown to me one night in a native hut, by a glimmering lamp; I in-stantly copied it, for fear of any difficulty arising, and then laid down ten francs on it, and told the owner to take which he pleased, the stone or the money; with a little hesitation at having the pleasure of hag-gling so cut short, he picked up the unexpected price. and I walked off behind the precious block to my house. The natives had so cleared out the earth from the heart of the town that all the Roman, Ptolemaic, and Persian houses and remains were gone; and the floor of the crater thus dug out consisted of the oldest

town, underlaid by a bed of ashes, which apparently
showed that the first settlement outside of the camp
was a cluster of mere booths. Here I found a scarab
factory, where they had made the scarabs of white
and blue paste, so well known in Greek cemeteries in

31. SCARAB MOULD AND SCARAB. 1 : 1.

Rhodes and elsewhere. Hundreds of earthenware
moulds and many scarabs were unearthed, and this
factory is the leading point for dating the early town.
The work of the scarabs is manifestly a Greek imitation of Egyptian style ; and the names of the kings

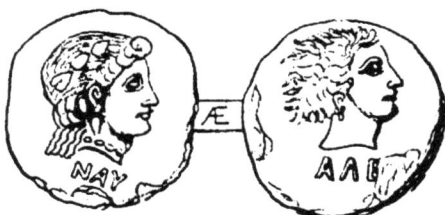

32. COIN OF NAUKRATIS. 1 : 1.

upon them show the dates to come down to the time
of Uah-ab-ra (Apries); but not a single example of
Amasis was found, proving the factory to have been ex-
tinct before his time. Probably the great defeat of the
Greek troops by Amasis was a severe blow to Greek

work for the time ; although Naukratis reaped the
benefit of the annihilation of the other Greek centres
(such as Defenneh), by being tolerated and having the
exclusive privilege of trade.   The first autonomous
coin of Naukratis yet known was found in the town ;
with heads of Naukratis and of the hero Alexander.

The old town had been so laid bare by the native
diggers, that it was possible to form a tolerable plan
of the streets and houses.   The street lines were
distinguished by the rubbish thrown out, mostly remains of food, shells, and bones ; while in later times,

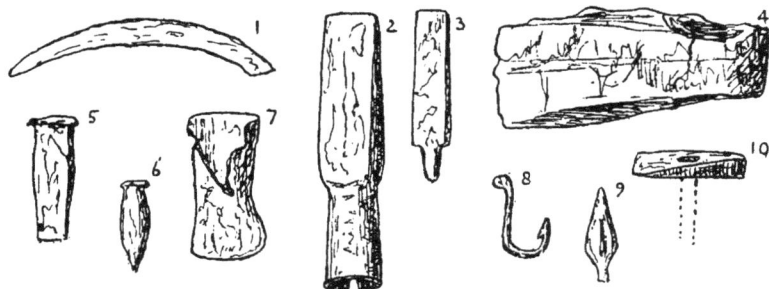

33. IRON TOOLS. 1, SICKLE ; 2, 3, CHISELS ; 4, AXE ; 5, 6, CHISELS ;
    7, AXE ; 8, FISH-HOOK ; 9, ARROW-HEAD ; 10, HAMMER.   1 : 8.

from the fifth century, the streets were regularly
mended with limestone chips and dust ; and often one
may trace the section of a puddle hole filled up with
chips and levelled.   Among the houses many fine
pieces of vases were found, and a small hoard of early
Greek silver coins and lumps of silver.   But the most
interesting matter was the history of tools, shown by
the variety of iron tools ; we here meet, for the first
time, what may be looked on as practically our modern
forms of chisels, &c. ; and we see what a debt we owe
to European invention, when we compare these with

the bronze tools of the Egyptians which preceded
them.

The cemetery has not yet been entirely found; a
portion of it, mainly of the Alexandrine age, was
cleared by Mr. Gardner, on a low mound to the north
of the town, alongside of the canal; but it was not
rich, and the principal objects were the Medusa heads,
moulded in terra cotta, which were affixed to the
wooden coffins. Probably the greater part of it is
beneath the modern village.

The potteries of Naukratis were famous in the time
of Athenaios, and long before that also, as we see by
the great heaps of burnt earth and potters' waste, and
by the distinctive style of much of the early pottery.
On comparing the characteristic styles of this place
with those of Defenneh, also inhabited by Greeks of
the same period, it is plain that most of the vases
found were made here by a local school of potters.
And though the clay is apparently of Greek origin,
yet it would be immeasurably easier to import a ton
of clay as ballast in a boat, than to move about a
thousand brittle and bulky vases.

We will now sum up the results of this discovery, in
its general connection with other antiquities. The
site now found fills a gap in Egyptian geography;
and it shows us how the Greeks were posted near the
capital of that age,—Sais, but toward the Libyan
frontier, where defence was needed; moreover they
dwelt on a canal, which could be used by Greek
traders at all seasons of the year, and which kept
them apart from the Egyptians on the Nile. The
plan of the town shows the fort, which became the

Panhellenion, with a settlement extending along the bank of the canal for half a mile below it; amidst which stood the temples of the separate external colonies of traders, Milesian, Samian, and Aeginetan.

34. NEGRO ON NAUKRATITE VASE.

The dedications found on the vases have been much discussed; but, viewed in the light of the history of the town, they are generally agreed now to be probably the earliest Ionic writing yet known. The styles of the vases made here are now fixed, and those found in other places which were exported from here can be identified; similarly we now know the source of the paste scarabs of mock-Egyptian design, often found in Greek tombs. The history of vase-painting

35. NAUKRATITE DESIGN. 1 : 4.

is assisted by the successive periods of the layers of the Apollo remains, which extend over what was a doubtful age; and the history of tools and of Greek manufactures has been much extended. On almost

every side this fresh view of the early sojourn of the
Greeks in Egypt has consolidated and enlarged our
knowledge ; and given for the first time an actual
insight into three centuries most important in their
bearing on Greek development, and for which we
were entirely dependent hitherto on literature and
tradition.

36. PART OF EMBOSSED GOLD BAND. ABOUT 70 A.D.   1 : 2.

37. RUINS OF DAPHNAE, IN THE DESERT.

CHAPTER IV.

DAPHNAE—TAHPANHES.

1886.

WHEN I was exploring in the marshy desert about Tanis, I saw from the top of a mound—Tell Ginn—a shimmering grey swell on the horizon through the haze; and that I was told was Tell Defenneh, or rather Def'neh, as it is called. It was generally supposed to be the Pelusiac Daphnae of Herodotos, and the Tahpanhes of the Old Testament; but nothing definite was known about it, and as it lies in the midst of the desert, between the Delta and the Suez Canal, twelve miles from either, it was not very accessible. After working at Tell Nebesheh for some time, I left it in Mr. Griffith's hands, and told my men that I wanted to work at Defneh; immediately I had more volunteers than I could employ, and I went into the desert to the work with a party of forty,—men, boys and girls,—and formed a settlement which enlarged up to seventy. We pitched on the old Pelusiac branch, which is now rather brackish, and it was sometimes difficult to drink the water : the people, however, made the best of it, and I never had a pleasanter time with my men than the two months I lived there, independent of all the local authorities which are generally met with. No one was allowed about the camp except the workers, and I never had the least trouble with them, nor heard a single squabble.

On reaching the place I found a wide flat plain bordering on the river, strewn all over with pottery, and with a mound of mud-brick building in the midst of it. I asked the name of the mound, and was told *Kasr Bint el Yehudi*, 'the palace of the Jew's daughter.' This at once brought Tahpanhes to my mind. Can there be any tradition here? I thought. I turned to Jeremiah, and there read how he came, with Johanan, the son of Kareah, and all the officers, and the king's daughters, down to Tahpanhes and dwelt there. We can hardly believe that the only place in Egypt where a celebrated daughter of a Jewish king lived, was called in later times 'the palace of the Jew's daughter' by accident, especially as such a name is only known here. Rather has this unique name clung to the place, as so many names have lasted, as long or longer, in Egypt and Syria. The next question was, if any reason could be found for its possessing a Greek name, Daphnae. Soon this was settled by finding an abundance of Greek pottery of the archaic period ; and so many Greek remains, and so little Egyptian, that it was evident a Greek camp had been here. This then was the camp of the Ionians described by Herodotos as having been founded by Psametichos I on the Pelusiac branch ; and on reaching down to the foundation of the fort, I there took out the tablets with the name of **Psamtik I**

as the founder.   But Herodotos relates a tale about
Sesostris having been attacked here by treachery,
suggesting that buildings had existed here in Ramesside times; and beneath some work of Psamtik I
found part of a wall of baked bricks, such as were
used in tombs at Tell Nebesheh, not far from this,
and only in Ramesside times.   Literature and discovery therefore go hand in hand here remarkably
closely.

This place then appears to have been an old fort on

38. Restoration of the Fort, showing the Large Platform
before the Entry.

the Syrian frontier guarding the road out of Egypt;
and here Psamtik settled part of his ' brazen men from
the sea,' and built a great fortress and camp, the twin
establishment to that of the rest of the Greek mercenaries at Naukratis, on the Libyan side.   The fort
was a square mass of brickwork, with deep domed
chambers or cells in it, which were opened from the
top ; this sustained the actual dwellings at about forty
feet above the plain, so that a clear view of the distant

towns and the desert could be seen over the camp wall, to some ten or twenty miles. The camp was defended by a wall forty feet thick, and probably as high; but this is now completely swept away down to the ground by the winds and rains. Beneath each corner of the fort was placed a set of plaques of various materials, both metals and stones, with the name of Psamtik, and at the south-west corner were

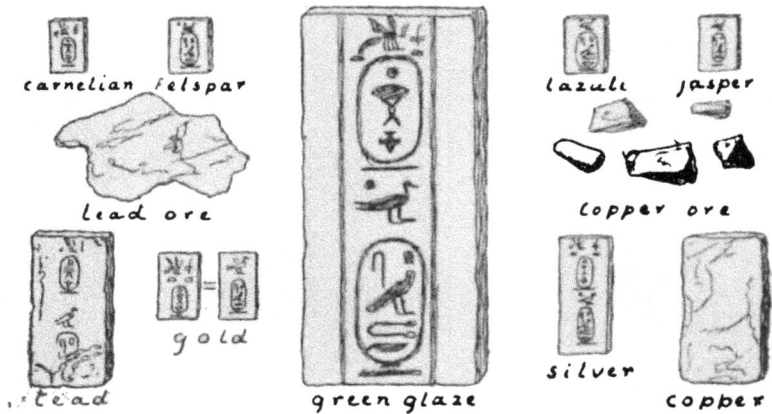

carnelian felspar lazuli jasper

lead ore copper ore

gold

stead green glaze silver copper

39. FOUNDATION DEPOSIT. 1 : 2.

also the bones of a sacrifice and other ceremonial deposits. This fort was enlarged by chambers added to it during a couple of generations later; and it must have been over that threshold which still lies in the doorway that the Jewish fugitives entered, when Hophra gave them an asylum from the Assyrian scourge. We cannot doubt that Tahpanhes—the first place on the road into Egypt—was a constant refuge for the Jews during the series of Assyrian invasions; especially as they met here, not the exclusive

Egyptians, but a mixed foreign population, mostly Greeks. Here then was a ready source for the introduction of Greek words and names into Hebrew, long before the Alexandrine age ; and even before the fall of Jerusalem the Greek names of musical instruments, and other words, may have been heard in the courts of Solomon's temple.

Another remarkable connection with the account given by Jeremiah was found on clearing around the fort. The entrance was in the side of a block of building projecting from the fort ; and in front of it, on the opposite side of its roadway, similarly projecting from the fort, was a large platform or pavement of brickwork (see fig. 38), suitable for out-door business, such as loading goods, pitching tents, &c.,—just what is now called a *mastaba*. Now Jeremiah writes of 'the pavement (or brickwork) which is at the entry of Pharaoh's house in Tahpanhes' (chap. xliii. 9, R.V.) ; this passage, which has been an unexplained stumbling-block to translators hitherto, is the exact description of the *mastaba* which I found ; and this would be the most likely place for Nebuchadrezzar to pitch his royal tent, as stated by Jeremiah.

The Greek vases found here show us an entirely new type, derived from the form of the Egyptian metal vases, but with the pointed base replaced by a circular foot. The painting and style of these vases are also unknown elsewhere, and were never found at Naukratis, so that it is certain that they were made by Daphniote potters. Several other styles of vases are found here, but it is very remarkable to note the total difference from the pottery of Naukratis. If the vases had been mainly imported to these settlements in Egypt, we should certainly find the remains much alike in two towns both occupied by Ionians at the same period, and probably trading with the same places; whereas every style that is most common at either of these towns is almost or entirely unknown at the other town. Such a widespread distinction shows

40. GREEK VASE, IMITATED FROM FORM OF EGYPTIAN METAL VASE.

how largely the pottery was made by local schools of potters, at the place where we find it, and how little of it was carried by trade.

The decoration of some of the vases is surprising, as showing at what an early date some patterns were used. On one vase are two bands of design, one of the archaic square volute, and the other of the lotus or

'palmetto' pattern, which would otherwise have been
supposed to be a century later.

The greater part of the vase fragments were found
in two chambers of the out-buildings of the fort.
These rooms had been standing unused by the Greeks,

41. VASE WITH DIFFERENT PATTERNS.

and served for rubbish holes, so that when we cleared
them out every scrape of the earth brought up some
painted fragments, and the lucky workmen who had
these places filled basket after basket each day. The
finest vase of all was found alone, in a passage on
the north of the fort, and nearly every fragment

was secured, ninety-nine pieces in all; it had been very probably a present to the Egyptian governor,

42. GREAT VASE; SUBJECTS, BOREAS AND TYPHON.

or possibly to the king on some visit there, as it

had traces of an inscription in demotic written on
it with ink.

The ground of the camp also supplied us with a
large number of things; for although it would hardly
be worth while to dig over so many acres exhaus-
tively, yet the ground had been so much denuded that
the surface-dust·was rich in small objects. I there-

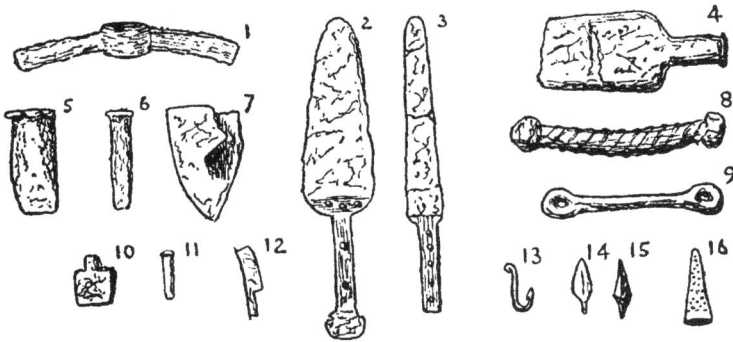

43. IRON TOOLS. 1, PICK; 2, 3, KNIVES; 4, AXE; 5, 6, CHISELS;
7, COULTER?; 8, 9, HORSES' BITS; 10, 11, CHISELS; 12 KNIFE;
13, FISH HOOK; 14, 15, ARROW-HEADS; 16, RASP. 1 : 12.

fore had it scraped over, and found hundreds of arrow-
heads of iron and bronze, iron scale armour, swords,
&c. One curious find was turned up the last afternoon
of the work; a large lot of cut-up lumps of silver, and
a massive gold handle off a tray, with lotus ' palmetto '
design; it had been violently wrenched off, and the
question is where would a soldier have a chance of
looting such valuable gold plate of Egyptian design?
It seems not unlikely that it was part of the royal
treasure of Apries, plundered ·on his overthrow by

Amasis. Another unusual object was picked up by one of the workmen on the surface (see Fig. 47, end of chapter); it appeared to be a little silver box with a sliding lid. The lid was slightly opened, and the feet of a gold figure showed inside it. As it could not be opened more without breaking it, I carefully cracked out one side, and took from it a most beautiful little statuette of Ra, hawk-headed, and then restored the case again. It had evidently been a shrine to wear on a necklace, as there was a loop at the back of the box.

Although all the stone buildings had been destroyed, and lines of chips alone remained to show the sandstone and limestone of their construction, yet the larger part of a great stele of sandstone still lies there, bearing a long hieroglyphic inscription. It is evident therefore that Egyptian interests were not neg-

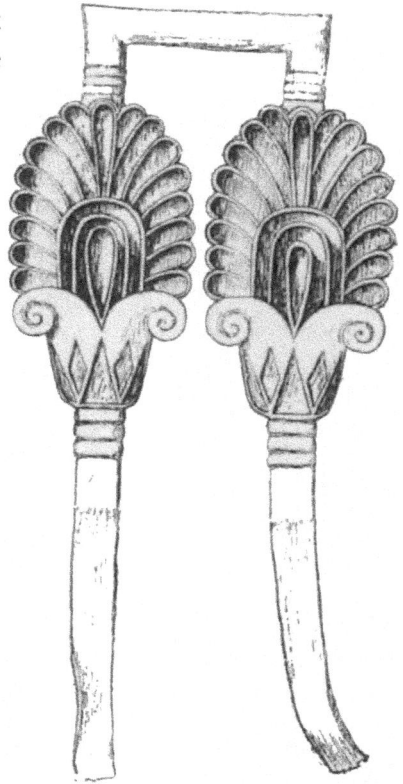

44. GOLD HANDLE.

lected, and that there must have been both Egyptian and Greek living side by side, together with Phoenician and Jew. One curious class of Egyptian remains

has given us the dates of some parts of the building ;
for the plaster sealings of the wine jars bear the
cartouches of the king, and they were most likely
knocked off and thrown aside within a few years of
being sealed. One room seemed to have belonged
to the royal butler, for dozens of plaster sealings
of Psamtik were found together there. A jar had
been fraudulently opened by boring through the

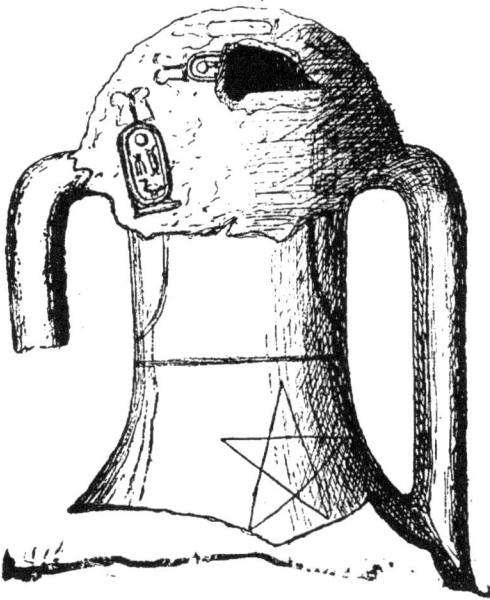

45. SEALED JAR NECK, WITH NAME OF AMASIS.

plaster, and the pottery stopper below it, and then
stopping the hole with fresh plaster. The prudent
butler had struck off the whole neck of the jar, so as
to preserve the proofs of the theft entire. The
particularity of the sealing is remarkable; first the

pottery bung was tied down, and the string sealed on clay by six inspectors; then a plaster cap was put over all that, and marked with the royal cartouche in several places.

The ruin of all this community came suddenly. Apries trusted to the Greek mercenaries, and defied the old Egyptian party (if indeed he was king at all according to Egyptian law); and Amasis, who had married the royal princess (and who was therefore a legal ruler), took the national side, and ousted his brother-in-law. Civil war was the consequence, and the Greeks—though straining all their power—were completely crushed by Amasis. He then carried out the protective policy of Egypt, and depopulated Daphnae, and all other Greek settlements excepting Naukratis, which latter thus became the only treaty-port open to Greek merchants. Hence, as we can date the founding of Defenneh almost to a year, about 665 B.C., when Psamtik established his mercenary camps, so we can also date its fall to a year in 564 B.C. when Amasis struck down the Greek trade. And this just accords with what we find, as there is a sudden cessation of Greek pottery at a stage some-way before the introduction of red figured ware, which took place about 490 B.C.

It appears likely that as Naukratis was the home of the scarab trade to Greece, so Daphnae was the home of the jewellery trade, and the source of the semi-Egyptian jewellery so often found in Greek tombs. Much evidence of the goldsmith's work was discovered; pieces of gold ornaments, pieces partly wrought, globules and scraps of gold, and a profusion

of minute weights, such as would only be of use for
precious metals.

We see then that Daphnae is the complement of
Naukratis: they were twin cities, and teach us even
more by their contrasts than their resemblances. We
again reach back, as at Naukratis, through the pre-

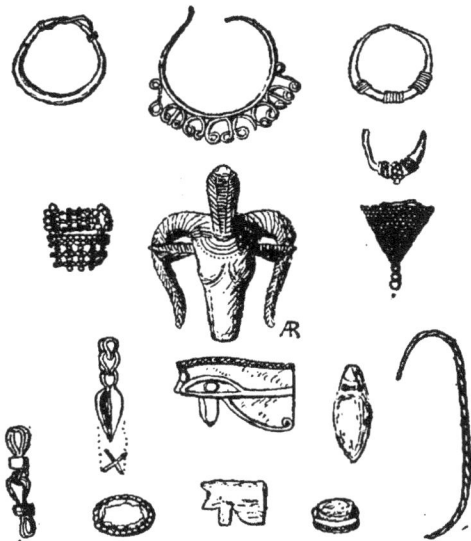

46. DAPHNIOTE GOLD WORK.

Alexandrine period to the foundation of Greek power
in Egypt. We again find the interaction of Greek
and Egyptian civilization. We again see the rise of
a local school of pottery, and have the great advantage of its being confined to just a century, of which
we know the exact limits. On the Jewish side of the
history the arrangement of 'the king's house in
Tahpanhes' exactly explains the narrative; the very
name of the place ‘echoes the sojourn of the fugitive

heiresses of Judah; and a valuable light is thrown on the early contact of the Hebrew race with the language and thought of the Greeks with whom they here dwelt.

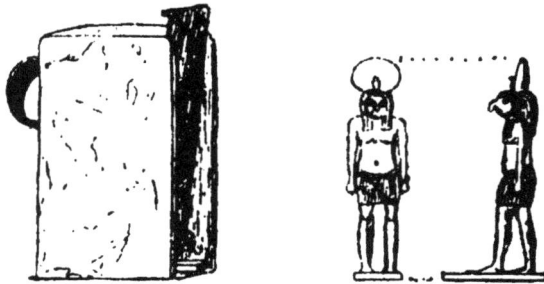

47. SILVER SHRINE, AND GOLD FIGURE OF RA.

48. GRANITE SHRINE OF TEMPLE.

CHAPTER V.

NEBESHEH.

1886.

WHILE living at Tanis I heard of a great stone, and
a cemetery, some miles to the south of that place, and
took an opportunity of visiting it. The site, Tell Nebesheh, is a very out-of-the-way spot; marshes and
canals cut it off from the rest of the delta; and the
only path to it from the cultivated region is across a
wide wet plain, on the other side of which is a wind-
ing bank hidden among the reeds of the bogs, and
only to be found by a native. After leaving Naukratis I went to this place, to try to clear up its history; and Mr. Griffith finished the work here, after I
had moved on to fresh discoveries. The great stone
was seen to be a monolith shrine, and therefore
probably a temple lay around it. As I walked over
the mounds, I saw that the tufts of reedy grass came
to an end along a straight line, the other side of which
was bare earth. This pointed out the line of the en-

closing wall of the temple, which I soon tracked round
on all sides. In the middle of one side the mound
dipped down, and a few limestone chips lay about.
Here I dug for the entrance pylon, and before long we
found the lower stones of it left in position; on clearing it out a statue of Ramessu II, larger than life, was
found, and fragments of its fellow; also a sphinx,
likewise in black granite, which had been so often re-
appropriated by various kings, that the original maker
could hardly be traced. Probably of the twelfth
dynasty to begin with, it had received a long inscription around the base from an official (the importance of
which we shall see presently), and later on six other
claimants seized it in succession. Outside of the
pylon there had been an approach, of which one ornament remained; this is an entirely fresh design, being
a column without any capital, but supporting a large
hawk overshadowing the king Merenptah, who kneels
before it. The sides of the column are inscribed.

The ground all around the monolith shrine was dug
over by us. Directly beneath the shrine the granite
pavement and its substructure remains entire; but
over the rest of the area only the bed of the foundation can be traced, all the stone having been removed.
Near the place of the entrance lay the throne of a
statue of Usertesen III, probably one of a pair by the
door, and showing that a temple had existed as far
back as the twelfth dynasty. The foundation deposits
in the corners I had to get out from beneath the water;
they were plaques of metals and stones, with the
name of Aahmes Si-nit, and pottery, showing that the
temple had been built in the twenty-sixth dynasty.

Among the ruins was found part of the black granite statue of the goddess Uati, which had doubtless stood in the monolith shrine as the great image of the temple.

Gold   Silver.

Green Glaze

49. FOUNDATION DEPOSIT. 1 : 2.

At the back of the shrine lay a black granite altar of Usertesen III, which, like the sphinx, had received an inscription by an official at a later time. These added inscriptions are of value, although they have been nearly effaced by subsequent kings ; they show that in the dark times before the eighteenth dynasty (for by their rudeness they fall in that age), certain royal chancellors could venture to usurp the monuments of previous kings. This could hardly have been possible if the king of that period cared for the monuments ; and we probably see in these chancellors the native viziers of the Hyksos kings, who were also apparently reckoned by the Egyptians as their rulers, and entered with ephemeral reigns of a year or two in the lists of the fourteenth dynasty. It was this vice-royalty that was conferred on Joseph, when the royal signet was given to him, and he had the honour of the second chariot.

But it was evident that some temple had existed

here before Aahmes, as the monuments were of earlier
ages; and on looking at the plan it is seen that his
temple is not in the middle of the enclosure, nor is it
in the line of the axis, but at right angles to it. I
therefore searched for the first temple about the midst
of the area, but for a long time nothing appeared besides chips. At last a mass of sand was found with a
vertical face, and this I at once recognised as the sand

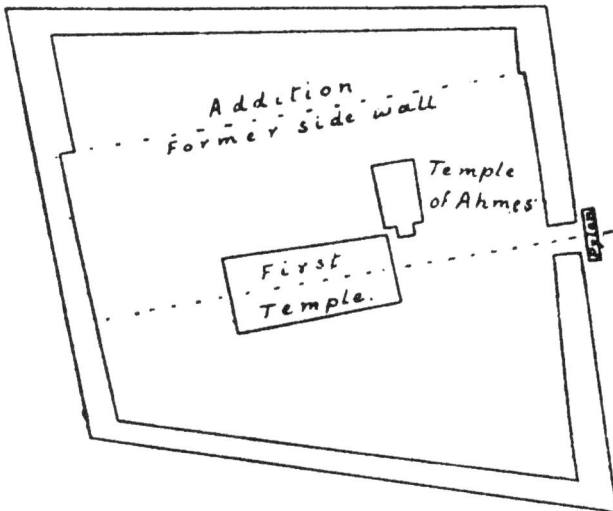

50. SANCTUARY AND TEMPLES.

bed laid in the earth, on which the walls of the temple
had been founded. It was covered with about twelve
feet of dust and chips, but by sinking pits at intervals
it was traced all round the whole extent of the former temple. The foundation deposits were unattain-
able, as they were too deep beneath the water level,
and the great sand bed collects the water so readily
that it could not be kept down more than three feet
by baling.

The cemetery was the other object at this place.
It proved to be of tolerable extent, about half a mile
long ; but the earliest tomb found was of Ramesside
age. Most of the burials were of the twenty-sixth to the
thirtieth dynasties, and the rarity of earlier interments
was explained by the condition of those which remain. The tomb chambers were all subterranean, yet
most of them were found roofless, though level with
the ground ; of some, only a few bricks remained at
the sides ; very few were still complete with a brick

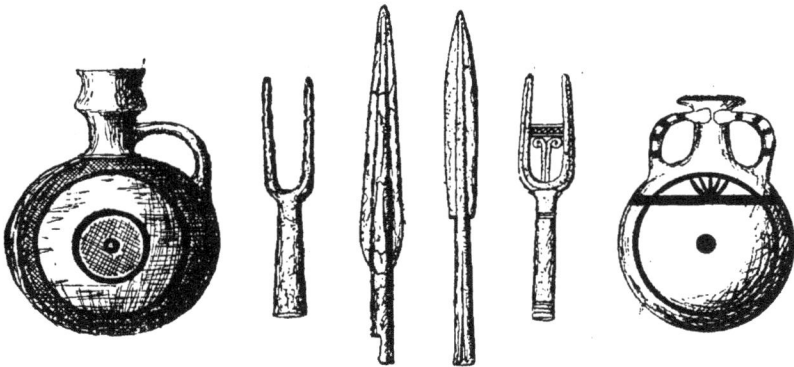

51. LYKAONIAN SPEARHEADS AND VASES.

vault. In fact they were in every stage of removal,
owing to the denudation of the sand ground in which
they were placed. The inference is only too evident,
that the earlier tombs have simply been denuded
wholly away, below the last brick of the walls. Many
of the chambers were excavated, but only in a few of
them were any ushabti figures found. Some of them
were sumptuous buildings of limestone ; but mostly
they were of the mud bricks, both in the walls and the

arched roofing. The most interesting class were those of Lykaonian mercenaries ; most likely from an out-post of the Daphnae camp, stationed here. In those tombs there were no ushabtis ; the bodies lay north and south, instead of east and west, as in the Egyptian tombs ; there were bronze and sometimes iron spear-heads, and curious forked spear-heads, like that on a funeral stele at Iconium ; and moreover, Cypriote pottery, generally pilgrim bottles.

While working in the cemetery we found one un-rifled tomb, containing four mummies, with their sets of amulets intact. These I carefully took off the bodies, noting the position of every object, so that I could afterwards rearrange them in their original order exactly as found. But the greatest discovery here in point of size was a great tomb formed by a ᐧ brick-walled yard or enclosure sunk in the ground. Within this were two limestone sarcophagi inscribed, and a splendid basalt sarcophagus, highly wrought, and with a long inscription ; this was encased in a huge block of limestone for protection, and it required much work to break this away when Count D'Hulst removed it to London. These sarcophagi were for a family who held offices in the Egyptian town of Am ; another sarcophagus found near these also named Am, and a piece of a statuette from the temple gave the same name. From these many different sources it appears that Am was the name of Tell Nebesheh ; especially as Uati was the goddess of Am, and hers was the statue of the great shrine and temple here. This gives a fresh point in the geography of ancient Egypt, and explains what Herodotos means by the Arabian

Buto, in contrast to the other Buto (or 'Temple of Uati') in the western half of the delta.

52. USHABTI FIGURES, TWENTIETH DYNASTY.   1 : 8.

53. A NILE MORNING.

CHAPTER VI.

UP THE NILE.

1887.

WHEN in the end of 1886 I went to Egypt, I had no excavations in prospect, having bid good-bye to the Fund; but I had promised to take photographs, for the British Association, and I had much wished to see Upper Egypt in a more thorough way than during a hurried dahabiyeh trip to Thebes in 1882. To this end my friend Mr. Griffith joined me. We hired a small boat with a cabin at Minia, and took six weeks wandering up to Assuan, walking most of the way in and out of the line of cliffs. Thus we saw much that is outside of the usual course, and spent afterwards ten days at Assuan, and three weeks at Thebes, in tents. On coming down the Nile I walked along the eastern shore from Wasta to Memphis, but found it a fruitless region. Lastly, I lived several weeks at Dahshur, for surveying the pyramids there.

Assuan proved a most interesting district, teeming with early inscriptions cut on the rocks ; and to copy all of these was a long.affair. Every day we went out with rope-ladder, bucket, and squeeze-paper, as early as we could, and returned in the dusk ; so at last some two hundred inscriptions were secured, many of which were of importance, and quite unnoticed before. These carvings are some of them notices of royal affairs, but mostly funereal lists of offerings for the benefit of various deceased persons. They abound most in the eleventh, twelfth, and thirteenth dynasties, though some of them are later ; and one records queen Amenardus, and another Psamtik II, of the twenty-sixth dynasty. Their main interest is in the great number of personal names which they preserve, and the relationships stated. We see that the father is often not named at all, and the father's family is scarcely ever noticed ; while on the mother's side the relations extend even to second cousins. To decipher these records is sometimes a hard matter, when they are very rudely chipped—or rather bruised —on the rough granite rocks ; and continually we used to consult and dispute about some sign for long enough to copy all the rest of the inscription. Some of them are, however, beautifully engraved, and quite monumental in style. The most striking, perhaps, is a rock on the island of Elephantine, which had never been noticed before, although in the pathway. It was a sort of royal album begun by Ra-kha-nefer (fifth dynasty); followed by Unas (fifth), who carved a handsome tablet. Then Ra-meri Pepi (sixth) appropriated Ra-kha-nefer's inscription; Ra-nefer-ka Pepi next carved a tablet; in later times, of the eleventh dynasty, Antef-aa II followed with another tablet; and lastly Amenemhat I (twelfth dynasty) placed the sixth inscription here.

54. TABLETS OF KINGS, FIFTH TO TWELFTH DYNASTIES. 1 : 40.

Not only were there these granite inscriptions to be copied, but also a great number of *graffiti* and travellers' names on the sandstone rocks, principally at Gebel Silsileh. Among these was a Phoenician inscription, one of the very few known in Egypt; and some curious quarry records of Roman age. The main inscription of this region is, however, one very seldom seen, even by antiquaries. as it is in a valley

55. AN INSCRIBED ROCK AT SILSILEH.

56. TABLET OF ANTEF AND MENTUHOTEP III.

where no one stops. It portrays Antef V and his vizier Khati worshipping Mentuhotep IV and his wife. Near it is another, smaller, tablet with the worship of the same king; and up the valley we discovered a tablet with the worship of Sankh-ka-ra, all of the eleventh dynasty. All over this district are many rude figures of animals, marked on the rocks by hammering: they are of various ages, some perhaps modern, but the earlier ones certainly before the eighteenth dynasty; and, to judge by the weathering of the rock, it seems probable that they were begun here long before any of the monuments of Egypt that we know. The usual figures are of men, horses, and boats, but there are also camels, ostriches and elephants to be seen.

57. ANIMAL FIGURES AT SILSILEH.

On the desert hills behind Esneh I found what is— so far—the oldest thing known from Egypt. In prehistoric days the Nile used to fill the whole breadth of the valley, to a depth of a couple of hundred feet, fed with the heavy rainfall that carved back the valleys all along the river by great waterfalls, the precipices of which now stand stark and arid in the bleaching sun. In those days flourished the forests, which lie now silicified in the silent desert. At Esneh the desert hills are several miles from the Nile, and on a spur of one—where probably no man sets foot for cen-

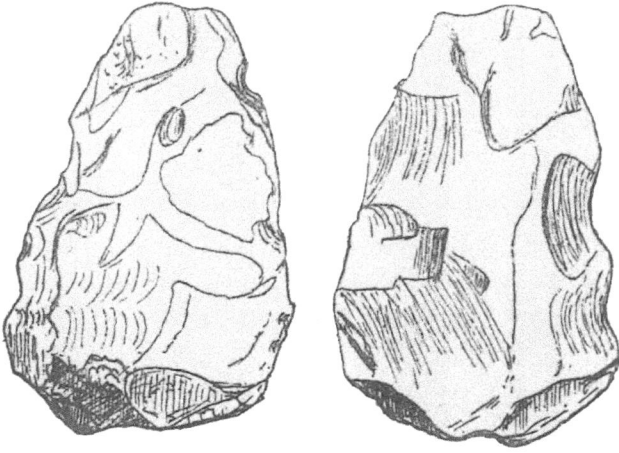

58. Oldest Tool in Egypt. 1:2.

59. People of Pun, S. Arabia

turies at a time—I found lying a palaeolithic wrought flint. It was about·a couple of hundred feet above the Nile, and being clearly a river-worn object, it had been left there in the old time of the Great Nile. The flints found by General Pitt-Rivers at Thebes belong to a later age, when the Nile had fallen to almost its present level. But those are far older than

60. HANEBU, EARLY GREEK.

any monuments known to us. We see then two stages before the beginning of what we can call history.

At Thebes my main work was in obtaining casts and photographs of all the types of foreign races on the monuments. For making ethnographical comparisons we were, until then, dependent on drawings, which were often incorrect. Now we have nearly two hundred photographs, all with the same size of head, giving several examples of each race that was represented by the Egyptians.

In most cases it would have been difficult to photograph the sculptures directly, owing to the difficulties of placing the camera, and the exact time of the

61. ENTRANCE OF SOUTH PYRAMID. CASING DESTROYED BELOW IT.

day required for the oblique sunlight.   Paper squeezes were therefore taken in preference, and a box of these, weighing a few pounds, served as moulds for producing in England a set of plaster casts which weighed a hundred times as much.   By waxing the paper several successive casts can be made from one mould, and from a set of the casts I took photographs, which can be printed interminably, and which are far more clear and distinct than if they were made directly from the stained and darkened sculptures. The paintings were of course photographed directly; where near the outer air enough light was obtained by reflectors of tinned plate; but in distant interiors, such as the tombs of the kings, an explosion of the proper amount of magnesium powder, mixed with chlorate of potash, gave excellent results for light.

Having finished the Theban work, I then went to

62. NORTH PYRAMID, AND SOUTHERN IN DISTANCE.

Dahshur, and there made a survey around the two large pyramids; but unfortunately I could not obtain the permission to uncover the bases of the pyramids in time to measure more than the southern one. This pyramid is interesting, as it retains the original casing over most of it, and gives us some idea of what the other pyramids looked like before the plundering by Arabs, and perhaps older thieves. The outside is peculiar, as being of a steeper angle below than above, and hence it is often called the 'blunted pyramid.'

The results of the survey were that it was all designed in even numbers of cubits. The base was 360 cubits, the height 200, divided into 90 cubits steep, and 110 cubits of flatter slope. The space walled in around it was 100 cubits wide. Another small pyramid on the south of it was 100 cubits square.

While at Dahshur I also found an interesting point about the ancient roads. The road from Sakkara to the oasis of Ammon was marked out by banks of gravel swept up on either side, leaving a clear space 50 cubits wide. The other road from Sakkara to the Fayum was marked out by milestones all along, there being a larger tablet at each *schoenus*, or 4 miles, while at each 1000 cubits, or third of a mile, was a lesser pillar on a stone socket.

63. WAY-MARKS ON FAYUM ROAD.

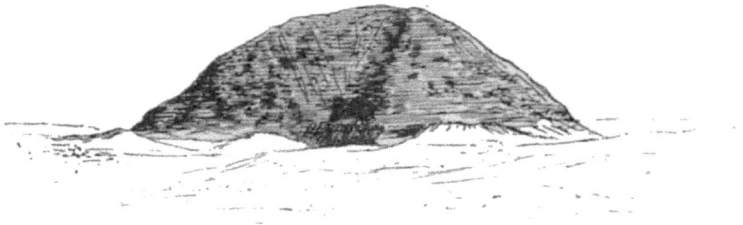

64. PYRAMID OF HAWARA.

CHAPTER VII.

HAWARA.

1888.

WHEN considering the places favourable for future excavations I had named Hawara and Illahun, amongst other sites, to M. Grébaut ; and he proposed to me that I should work in the Fayum province in general. The exploration of the pyramids of this district was my main object, as their arrangement, their date, and their builders were quite unknown. Hawara was not a convenient place to work at, as the village was two miles from the pyramid, and a canal lay between ; I therefore determined to form a camp of workmen to live on the spot, as at Daphnae. For this purpose I needed to recruit a party from a little distance, and began my work therefore at the ancient Arsinoe or Crocodilopolis, close to Medinet el Fayum. Here I cleared the pylon of the temple, of which a few disturbed blocks remain, and found a second mention of Amenemhat II beside that already known ; but his work

G

had all been altered and rebuilt, probably by Ramessu
II. Four or five different levels of building and
reconstruction could be traced, and
the depth of rubbish over the approach
to the temple in the shallowest part
of the mounds was twenty-four feet.
Within the great enclosure of mud-
brick wall, the site of the temple
could be traced by following the bed
of sand, on which the foundations
had been laid ; but scarcely a single
stone was left. One reused block
had a figure of a king of the nineteenth dynasty, probably Ramessu
II ; and this leads us to date as late
as Ptolemy II the temple which we
can trace here. He doubtless built
a large temple, as the place received
much attention in his time, and was
dedicated to his sister-wife Arsinoe ;
she was specially worshipped along
with the great gods, as we know from
the stele of Pithom. The only early
65. FLINT KNIFE. objects found here were flint knives
in the soil of the temple ; these belong to the twelfth
dynasty, as we know from later discoveries.

A short work of a few days at Biahmu resolved the
questions about the so-called pyramids there. So
soon as we began to turn over the soil we found chips
of sandstone colossi; the second day the gigantic
nose of a colossus was found, as broad as a man's
body; then pieces of carved thrones, and a fragment

of inscription of Amenemhat III. It was evident that the two great piles of stone had been the pedestals of

66. PEDESTALS OF BIAHMU.

colossal seated monolithic statues, carved in hard quartzite sandstone, and brilliantly polished. These

67. WALL OF COURT.

statues faced northward, and around each was a court-yard wall with sloping outer face, and red granite

G 2

gateway in the north front.   The total height of the
colossi was about sixty feet from the ground.   The
limestone pedestal rose twenty-one feet, then the sandstone colossus had a base of four feet, on which the
figure, seated on its throne, rose to a height of thirty-
five feet more.   Thus the whole statue and part of its
pedestal would be visible above the enclosing courtyard
wall, and it would appear from a distance as if it were

68. SECTION OF COURT, WITH STATUE.

placed on a truncated pyramid.   The description of
Herodotos, therefore, is fully accounted for; and it
shows that he actually saw the figures, though from a
distance, as any person who visited them closely
would not have described them in such a manner.

Having by this time formed and organised a good
body of workmen, I moved over to Hawara, with as
many men as I wanted ; and the only difficulty was
to restrain the numbers who wished to work.   The
pyramid had never been entered in modern times, and

its arrangement was wholly unknown ; explorers had fruitlessly destroyed much of the brickwork on the north side, but yet the entrance was undiscovered. In Roman times the stone casing had been removed, and as the body of the structure was of mud bricks, it had crumbled away somewhat ; each side was therefore encumbered with chips and mud. After vainly searching the ground on the north side for any entrance, I then cleared the middle of the east side, but yet no trace of any door could be found. As it was evident then that the plan was entirely different to that of any known pyramid, and it would be a hopeless task to clear all the ground around it, I therefore settled to tunnel to the midst. This work was very troublesome, as the large bricks were laid in sand, and rather widely spaced ; hence as soon as any were removed, the sand was liable to pour out of the joints, and to loosen all the surrounding parts. The removal of each brick was therefore done as quietly as possible, and I had to go in three times a day and insert more roofing boards, a matter which needed far more skill and care than a native workman would use. After many weeks' work (for there was only room for one man), I found that we were halfway through, but all in brick. On one side of the tunnel, however, I saw signs of a built wall, and guessing that it had stood around the pit made for the chamber during the building, I examined the rock-floor, and found that it sloped down slightly, away from the wall. We turned then to the west, and tunnelling onwards, we reached the great roofing beams of the chamber in a few days. No masons of the district, however, could cut through them, and I had to leave the work till the next season. Then, after a further search on all the four sides for the entrance, the masons attacked the sloping stone roof, and in two or three weeks' time a hole beneath them was reported; anxiously I watched them enlarge it until I could squeeze through, and then I entered the chamber above the sepulchre; at one side I saw a lower hole, and going down I found a broken way into the sandstone sepulchre, but too narrow for my shoulders. After sounding the water inside it, a boy was put down with a rope-ladder; and at last, on looking through the hole, I could see by the light of his candle the two sarcophagi, standing rifled and empty. In a day or two we cleared away the rubbish from the original entrance passage to the chamber, and so went out into the passages, which turned and wandered up and down. These were so nearly choked with mud, that in many parts the only way along them was by lying flat, and sliding along the mud, pushed by fingers and toes. In this way, sliding, crawling, and wading, I reached as near to the outer mouth of the passage as possible; and then by measuring back to the chamber, the position of the mouth on the outside of the pyramid was pretty nearly found. But so deep was it under the rubbish, and so much encumbered with large blocks of stone, that it took about a fortnight to reach it from the outside.

The pyramid had been elaborately arranged so as to deceive and weary the spoiler, and it had apparently occupied a great amount of labour to force an entrance. The mouth was on the ground level, on the south side, a quarter of the length from the south-west corner. The original explorers descended a passage with steps to a chamber, from which apparently there was no exit. The roof consisted of a sliding trap-door, however, and breaking through this another chamber was

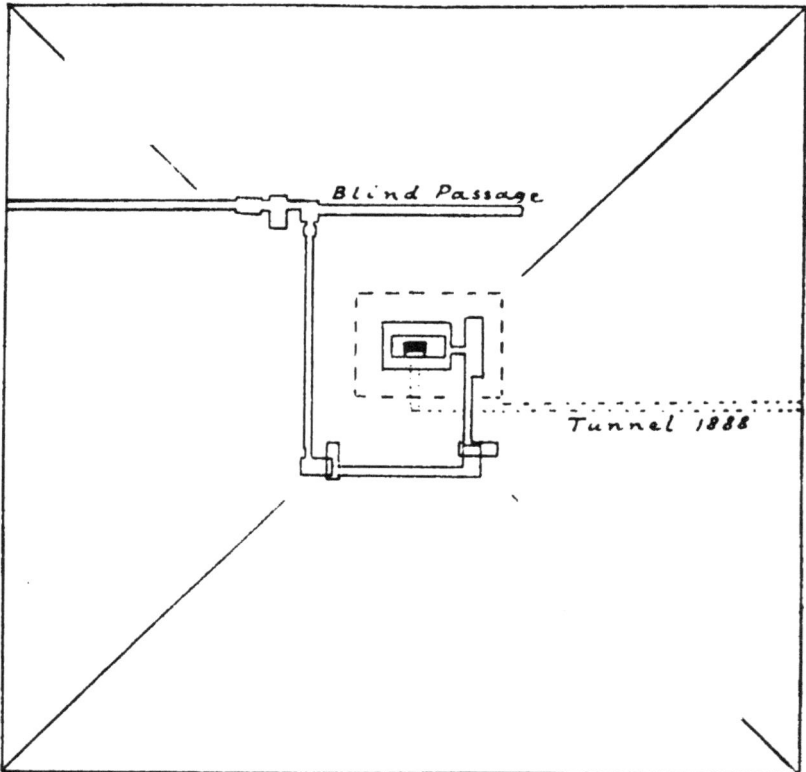

69. PLAN OF PYRAMID.

reached at a higher level. Then a passage opened to the east, closed with a wooden door, and leading to another chamber with a trap-door roof. But in front of the explorer was a passage carefully plugged up solid with stone ; this they thought would lead to the prize, and so all the stones were mined through, only to lead to nothing. From the second trap-door chamber a passage led northward to the third such chamber. From that a passage led west to a chamber with two wells, which seemed as if they led to the tomb, but both were false. This chamber also was almost filled with masonry, which all concealed nothing, but had given plenty of occupation to the spoilers who removed it in vain. A filled-up trench in the floor of the chamber really led to the sepulchre ; but arriving there no door was to be found, as the entrance had been by the roof, an enormous block of which had been let down into place to close the chamber. So at last the way had been forced by breaking away a hole in the edge of the glassy-hard sandstone roofing block, and thus reaching the chamber and its sarco-phagi. By a little widening of the spoilers' hole I succeeded in getting through it into the chamber. The water was up to the middle of my body, and so exploration was difficult ; but the floor was covered with rubbish and chips, which might contain parts of the funereal vessels, and therefore needed searching. The rubbish in the sarcophagi I cleared out myself ; and then I set some lads to gather up the scraps from the floor on the flat blade of a hoe (as it was out of arms' reach under water), and after searching them they threw them into the sarcophagi. Thus we anxiously worked on for any inscribed fragments ; my anxiety being for the cartouche of the king, the boys' anxiety for the big bakhshish promised, at *per* hiero-glyph found, extra value given for cartouches. The system worked, for in the first day I got the coveted

70. INSCRIPTION OF AMENEMHAT III.

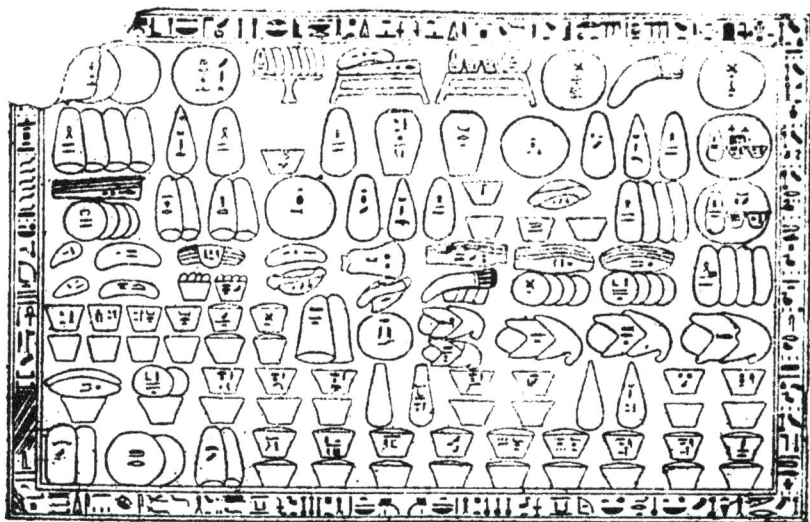

71. ALTAR OF NEFERU-PTAH.

prize, a piece of an alabaster vessel with the name of Amenemhat III, proving finally to whom the pyramid belonged ; and other parts of inscribed vessels were found. Still there was a puzzle as to the second sarcophagus, which had been built up between the great central one and the chamber side. On clearing in the chamber which led to the sepulchre, however, they found a beautiful altar of offerings in alabaster, covered with figures of the offerings all named, over a hundred in all, and dedicated for the king's daughter, Neferu-ptah ; near it were parts of several bowls in the form of half a trussed duck, also bearing her name : so doubtless the second interment was hers ; and she must have died during her father's life, and before the closing of the pyramid. Of the actual bodies I found a few scraps of charred bones, besides bits of charcoal and grains of burnt diorite in the sarcophagi ; also a beard of lazuli for inlaying was found in the chamber. The wooden inner coffins, inlaid with hard stone carving, had therefore been burnt. The chamber itself is a marvellous work ; nearly the whole height of it is carved out of a single block of hard quartzite sandstone, forming a huge tank, in which the sarcophagus was placed. In the inside it is twenty-two feet long and nearly eight feet wide, while the sides are about three feet thick. The surface is polished, and the corners so sharply cut that I mistook it for masonry, until I searched in vain for the joints. Of course it was above water level originally ; but all this region has been saturated by a high level canal of Arab times. Afterwards I had all the earth removed from the pyramid passages as far as practicable, but nothing further was found there. No trace of inscription exists on either the walls or sarcophagi ; and but for the funereal furniture, even the very name would not have been recovered.

Though the pyramid was the main object at Hawara, it was but a lesser part of my work there. On the south of the pyramid lay a wide mass of chips and fragments of building, which had long been generally identified with the celebrated labyrinth. Doubts, however, existed, mainly owing to Lepsius having considered the brick buildings on the site to have been part of the labyrinth. When I began to excavate the result was soon plain, that the brick chambers were built on the top of the ruins of a great stone structure ; and hence they were only the houses of a village, as they had at first appeared to me to be. But beneath them, and far away over a vast area, the layers of stone chips were found ; and so great was the mass that it was difficult to persuade visitors that the stratum was artificial, and not a natural formation. Beneath all these fragments was a uniform smooth bed of *beton* or plaster, on which the pavement of the building had been laid : while on the south side, where the canal had cut across the site, it could be seen how the chip stratum, about six feet thick, suddenly ceased, at what had been the limits of the building. No trace of architectural arrangement could be found, to help in identifying this great structure with the labyrinth : but the mere extent of it proved that it was far larger than any temple known in Egypt. All the temples of Karnak, of Luxor, and a few on the western side of Thebes, might be placed together within the vast space of these buildings at Hawara. We know from Pliny and others, how for centuries the labyrinth had been a great quarry for the whole district ; and its destruction occupied such a body of masons, that a small town existed there. All this information, and the recorded position of it, agrees so closely with what we can trace, that no doubt can now remain regarding the position of one of the wonders of Egypt.

The cemetery of Hawara was a great resource for discoveries, and it proved to be one of the richest fields that I have found, although it was entirely an unexpected prize. The oldest tombs, of the pyramid time, had all been ruined ages ago, and the pits reused for the nineteenth dynasty, the Ptolemaic times, and crocodile burial of the Roman age. But some slabs from the stone chapels on the surface had fallen down the tomb shafts, and were thus preserved.

The oldest unravaged tomb was of about the end of the twenty-sixth dynasty ; and that was a treasury of amulets, being the funeral vault of the family of a great noble, Horuta. It was half inundated, the water being thigh deep, and though all woodwork and stucco was spoilt, yet the amulets of stone, and some of pottery, were uninjured. The great interment was that of Horuta himself. In a side chamber, branching from the large chamber, a huge sarcophagus of hard and tough limestone had been placed, containing three successive coffins of wood. This was built in solidly with masonry all around it, filling up the whole chamber, so that its very existence was hardly to be suspected by anyone in the large chamber. To clear this out in such a position was hard work : a party of good hands were steadily labouring at it, mainly by contract, for two or three months. Down a well, forty feet deep, and in a pitch-black chamber, splashing about in bitter water, and toiling by candle-light, all the work had to be done ; and dragging out large blocks of masonry in a very confined space in such circumstances is slow and tedious. While thus mining the way to the expected burial, we lit on a hole in the masonry filled with large ushabtis standing in rows, two hundred in all, of the finest workmanship ; and, before long, on the other side of the sarcophagus. two hundred more were found in a similar recess. But the sarcophagus itself was most difficult to open. The lid block was nearly two feet thick, and almost under water. It was far too heavy for us to move entire, so some weeks were spent in cutting it in two. One piece was then raised, but it proved to be the foot end ; and though I spent a day struggling with the inner coffins, sitting in the sarcophagus up to my nose in water, I yet could not draw them out from under the rest of the stone lid. So after some days the men raised that, enough to get one's head in between the under side of it and the water ; and then I spent another gruesome day, sitting astride of the inner coffin, unable to turn my head under the lid without tasting the bitter brine in which I sat. But though I got out the first coffin lid, the inner one was firmly fastened down to its coffin ; and though I tried every way of loosening the coffin, it was so firmly set in a bed of sand that crowbars and mining with the feet were useless, and it was so

low in the water as to be out of arms' reach. The
need of doing everything by feeling, and the impos-
sibility of seeing what was done under the black water,
made it a slow business. A third day I then attacked
it, with a helpful friend, Mr. Fraser. We drilled holes
in the coffin, as it was uninscribed, and fixed in stout
iron bolts. Then, with ropes tied to them, all our
party hauled again and again at the coffin ; it yielded ;
and up came an immense black mass to the surface of
the water. With great difficulty we drew it out, as it
was very heavy, and we had barely room for it beneath
the low ceiling. Anxiously opening it, we found a
slight inner coffin, and then the body of Horuta
himself, wrapped in a network of beads of lazuli, beryl,
and silver, the last all decomposed. Tenderly we
towed him out to the bottom of the entrance pit,
handling him with the same loving care as Izaak his
worms. And then came the last, and longed-for scene,
for which our months of toil had whetted our appetites,
—the unwrapping of Horuta. Bit by bit the layers of
pitch and cloth were loosened, and row after row of
magnificent amulets were disclosed, just as they were
laid on in the distant past. The gold ring on the
finger which bore his name and titles, the exquisitely
inlaid gold birds, the chased gold figures, the lazuli
statuettes delicately wrought, the polished lazuli and
beryl and carnelian amulets finely engraved, all the
wealth of talismanic armoury, rewarded our eyes with
a sight which has never been surpassed to archaeological gaze. No such complete and rich a series of
amulets has been seen intact before ; and as one by
one they were removed all their positions were

recorded, and they may now be seen lying in their original order in the Ghizeh Museum. The rest of the family of Horuta lay in the large chamber, some in stone sarcophagi, some only in wooden coffins.

They also had their due funereal wealth; and a dozen other sets of amulets rewarded our search, some of them as fine a series as any known before, but not to compare for a moment with those of the walled-in patriarch.

Of rather later age, perhaps Ptolemaic, was a large wooden coffin that we found; the body and the lid were two equal parts, plainly rectangular; and they lay where some old spoiler had left them, separated, and afterwards buried

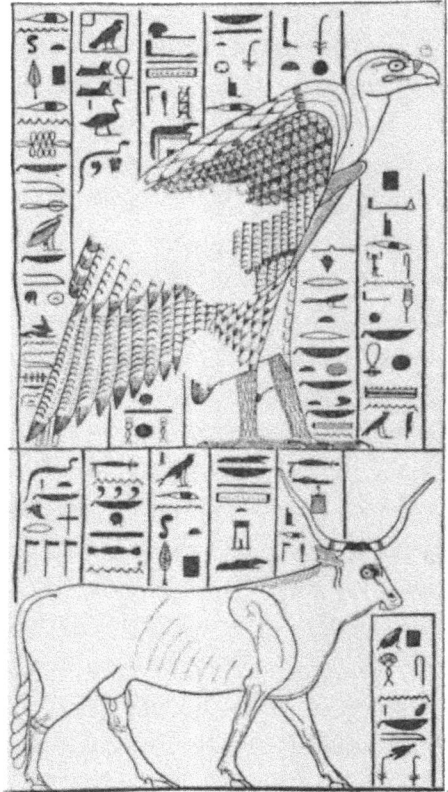

72. VULTURE AND COW, FROM COFFIN LID.

under a heap of stuff thrown out in digging later tombs. The whole surface of this sarcophagus was stuccoed, inside and outside, top and bottom, and every part of it finely painted and inscribed. The top of the lid had the deities of the district, the hawk, the Osiris-crocodile, and the bennu, with inscriptions; the lower part inside bore other animals, the vulture, the cow, and white hippopotamus; the inside of the lid had the two crocodile-headed Sebeks and the ape; and underneath the lower part, or body, was a long inscription, partly biographical. I had a terrifying experience with this coffin; when I found it much of the stucco was loose, and any amount of trouble was worth while to preserve so beautiful and important an object. I observed in copying it that parts had been waxed, to heighten the colour, and this suggested to me to fasten down the stucco by wax. I tried melting it on with a plate of hot iron, but could scarcely do it without blackening it with smoke. In course of this I poured a layer of wax over the surface; but what was my horror to see as the wax cooled that it contracted into saucer-formed patches, lifting up with it the stucco, and leaving bare wood beneath! To touch these wax patches must irrevocably ruin all hopes of replacing the stucco; so I covered it with sheets of paper, and thought on it for some days, a spectre of dismal failure. I tried in vain to buy a brazier at Medinet; so at last, making a grating of wire, I filled it with red-hot charcoal, and supported it over part of the unlucky coffin. As I watched it, the wax softened, flattened, and dropped exactly into place again; patch after patch settled down, the wax melted and ran in under the stucco; and at last I saw the whole surface completely relaid, and fixed so firmly that even the fearful rattle of an Egyptian railway wagon, in the long journey to Bulak, did not injure it.

But perhaps the greatest success at Hawara was in the direction least expected. So soon as I went there I observed a cemetery on the north of the pyramid; on digging in it I soon saw that it was all Roman, the remains of brick tomb-chambers; and I was going to give it up as not worth working, when one day a mummy was found, with a painted portrait on a wooden panel placed over its face. This was a beautifully drawn head of a girl, in soft grey tints, entirely classical in its style and mode, without any Egyptian influence. More men were put on to this region, and in two days another portrait-mummy was found; in two days more a third, and then for nine days not one; an anxious waiting, suddenly rewarded by finding three. Generally three or four were found every week, and I have even rejoiced over five in one day. Altogether sixty were found in clearing this cemetery, some much decayed and worthless, others as fresh as the day they were painted.

Not only were these portraits found thus on the mummies, but also the various stages of decoration that led up to the portrait. First, the old-fashioned stucco cartonnage coverings, purely Egyptian, of the Ptolemies. Next, the same made more solidly, and with distinct individual differences, in fact, modelled masks of the deceased persons. Then arms modelled in one with the bust, the rest of the body being covered with a canvas wrapper painted with mythologic scenes, all purely Egyptian. Probably under Hadrian the first portraits are found, painted on a canvas wrapper, but of Greek work. Soon the canvas was abandoned,

Late Ptolemaic

1st cent A.D

About 120-140 A.D.

About 150 to 250 A.D

73. FOUR STAGES OF MUMMY DECORATION.

and a wooden panel used instead ; and then the regular series of panel portraits extends until the decline in the third century. All this custom of decorating the mummies arose from their being kept above ground for many years in rooms, probably connected with the house. Various signs of this usage can be seen on the mummies, and in the careless way in which they were at last buried, after such elaborate decoration.

Though only a sort of undertaker's business, in a provincial town of Egypt, and belonging to the Roman age, when art had greatly declined, yet these paintings give us a better idea of what ancient painting was, and what a high state it must have reached in its prime, than anything yet known, excepting some of the Pompeian frescoes. Mannerism is evident in nearly all of these, and faults may be easily detected ; yet there is a spirit, a sentiment, an expression about the better examples which can only be the relic of a magnificent school, whose traditions and skill were not then quite lost. A few indeed of these heads are of such power and subtlety that they may stand beside the works of any age without being degraded. If such was Greek painting still, centuries after its zenith, by obscure commercial artists, and in a distant town of a foreign land, we may dimly credit what it may have been in its grandeur. The National Gallery now begins its history of paintings far before that of any other collection ; the finest examples left, after the selection of the Bulak Museum, being now at Trafalgar Square.

The technical methods of these paintings have been

much discussed. Certainly the colours were mixed with melted wax as a medium, and it seems most likely that both the brush and hard point were used. The backing is a very thin cedar panel, on which a coat of lead colour priming was laid, followed by a flesh-coloured ground where the face was to come. The drapery is freely marked in with bold brushfuls of colour, while the flesh is carefully and smoothly laid on with zigzag strokes. In some portraits the boldness of the work is almost like some modern romanticist's ; at a foot distance the surface is nearly incomprehensible, at six or eight feet it produces a perfect effect.

Several of these pictures when found were in a perilous state ; the film of wax paint was scaled loose from the panel, and they could never be even tilted up on edge without perishing. After finding several in this tender state, and pondering on their preservation, I ventured to try the same process as for the stucco coffin. The wire-grating was filled with red-hot charcoal, and then the frail portrait was slid in beneath it, a few drops of melted wax laid on it, and watched. In a few seconds the fresh wax began to spread, and then at once I ladled melted wax all over the surface ; a second too long, and it began to fry and to blister ; too sharp a tilt to drain it when it came out, and the new wax washed away the paint. But with care and management it was possible to preserve even the most rotten paintings with fresh wax ; and afterwards I extended this waxing to all substances that were perishable, woodwork and leather, as well as stucco and paint.

This custom, however, of preserving the mummies above ground, adorned with the portraits, gave way about the time of Constantine, or perhaps a little earlier, and immediate burial was adopted.   Probably this was partly due to the pro-
gress of Christianity.

Instead, therefore, of finding the portraits of the persons, we have their embroidered and richly woven garments ; for they were buried in the finest clothes they had when alive. And their possessions were buried with them.   In one grave was a lady's casket made of wood inlaid with ivory panels, on which figures were carved and coloured with in-laying.   The fine cut-glass vase from another grave is of the whitest glass, and excellently cut with the wheel ; perhaps the finest example of such work from Roman times.   The toys were also buried with the chil-dren, and dolls, with all their furniture, — bedstead, mirror, table, toilet-box, clothes-basket, and other paraphernalia—were

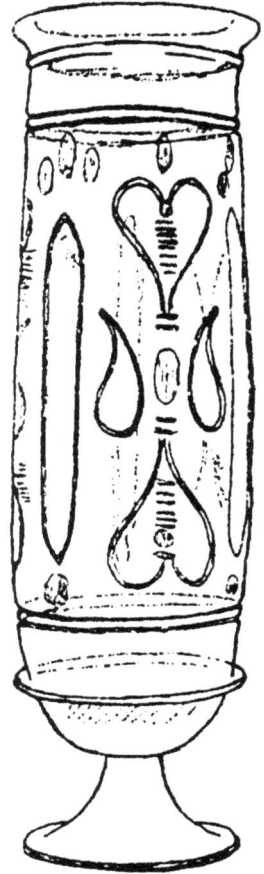

74. Cut-glass Vase.

placed with the little ones who had died.   Even more elaborate toys were laid here, such as the curious *terra cotta* of a sedan chair, borne by two porters, with a lady seated inside ; a loose figure that can be removed.

75. SIDE OF IVORY CASKET.   1 : 4.

76. SEDAN CHAIR, TERRA COTTA.   1 : 4.

In one instance a far more valuable prize accompanied a body ; under the head of a lady lay a papy-

rus roll, which still preserved a large part of the second
book of the Iliad, beautifully written, and with mar-
ginal notes. A great quantity of pieces of papyrus,
letters and accounts, of Roman age, were also found
scattered about in the cemetery. In a large jar buried
in the ground lay a bundle of title-deeds: they
recorded the sale of some monastic property, and
were most carefully rolled, bound up with splints of
reed, to prevent their being bent, and wrapped in
several old cloths.

1 : 6.   77. ROMAN RAG DOLLS.   1 : 4.

In yet another respect Hawara proved a rich field.
In the coffins, in the graves, and in the ruins of the
chambers, were still preserved the wreaths with which
the dead had been adorned, and the flowers which the
living had brought to the tombs. These wreaths were
often in the most perfect condition, every detail of the

flowers being as complete as if dried for a herbarium. They illustrate the accounts of Pliny and other writers about ancient wreaths, and the plants used for them, and show what a careful and precise trade the wreath-maker's was. Beside the decorative plants there were many seeds, and remains of edible fruits and vegetables, which had been left behind in the surface chambers of the tombs after the funereal feasts. Altogether, the cemetery of Hawara has doubled the extent of our list of ancient Egyptian botany, under the careful examination given by Mr. Newberry to the boxes full of plants which I brought away.

Few places, then, have such varied interest as Hawara ; the twelfth dynasty pyramid, the labyrinth, the amulets of Horuta, the portraits, the botany, and the papyri, are each of special interest and historical value.

In this year also I visited the other side of the lake of the Fayum, now known as the Birket Kerun. There, at some miles back in that utter solitude, stands a building of unknown age and unknown purport. It is massively constructed, but without any trace of inscription, or even ornament, which would tell its history. That it cannot be as late as the Kasr Kerun, is probable from its being at a much higher level. There would be no object in making a building at some miles distant in the desert, as it now is ; and we must rather suppose it to belong to the age when the lake was full, and extended out so far. But where it comes before the Ptolemaic age we cannot say. The front doorway leads into a long court, which has a chamber at each end, and seven recesses in the long

78. BUILDING NORTH OF BIRKET KERUN.

79. INTERIOR OF BUILDING.

side opposite the entrance. These recesses have had
doors, of which the pivot holes can be seen. There

are no traces of statues or of sarcophagi about; and the place has been keenly tunnelled and explored by treasure-seekers.

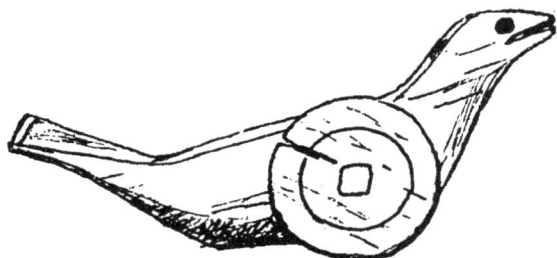

80. TOY BIRD ON WHEELS, HAWARA.

81. PYRAMID OF ILLAHUN.

CHAPTER VIII.

ILLAHUN.

1889-90.

HAVING finished opening the pyramid of Hawara, the next attraction was that of Illahun, a few miles to the east of it, in the Nile valley, at the entrance to the Fayum. This pyramid differs from all others in that the lower part is a natural rock cut into shape ; upon that a mass of mud-brick rises, like that of Hawara, and around the base lie the fragments of the fine limestone casing which originally covered it. As almost all the pyramids had their chambers built in a sort of well in the rock base, I tried this pyramid on such an hypothesis, and therefore cleared the edge of its rocky portion all round as far as possible, to search for the cut into it, expected to lead to the excavation for the chamber. At the south-east corner this was difficult, as the rock was there deficient, and the core had been made up by layers of chips. Still, for months we went on clearing the sides and searching. Much other work was going on meanwhile, and by different sources I had found that the pyramid belonged to Usertesen II, as we shall notice presently. Amongst other work, I searched along a ledge in the rock at the base, where the pavement had originally been placed. While doing this we found a well, which I did not clear, as I was near the end of my season for work ; but, on Mr. Fraser coming to secure the place during my absence, I commended this well to his notice as a possible entrance. He cleared it out, and at forty feet deep found a passage leading up into the pyramid. Then it was evident that no other external sign on the pyramid itself was possible, for the passages and chambers were wholly cut in the rock, and the pyramid merely stood on the surface, without any connection with the sepulchre beneath it.

There were two well-entrances to the pyramid, close together. One beyond the pavement was so carefully covered with rubbish that I could not have found it unless I had made a great clearance ; by this the sarcophagus and large blocks of masonry were taken in. The smaller well was evidently for the workmen to gain access to the lower side of the blocks that were in course of being taken in : it was hidden by the pavement, was found anciently, and served for spoilers to enter by, and lastly was found again in my digging. Had it not been for this smaller well, I believe the pyramid would have been still inviolate.

The passage in the inside is rough hewn in the soft

rock, and was smeared over with a coat of thin plaster originally, but without a trace of ornament or inscription. It is wide, and high enough to walk upright freely. At the end it opened into a chamber lined with blocks of limestone, of which a large part has been removed, probably by the Ramesside masons, when they plundered the pyramid and its temples for stone. At the west end of this chamber, which runs east and west, is the door to a red granite chamber, containing the sarcophagus. This second chamber is roofed exactly like that of Menkaura's pyramid at Gizeh, with slanting blocks cut out in a curve below. The sarcophagus is one of the finest products of mechanical skill that is known from ancient times. It is of red granite, of a form not before met with, having a wide rectangular brim. The surfaces are all ground flat, but not polished; truth, and not effect, was sought for. And its errors of work in flatness and regularity are not more than the thickness of a visiting card. Its accuracy of proportion is also fine, as each dimension is a whole number of palms, with a fluctuation of only one part in a thousand. In front of the sarcophagus stood the alabaster table of offerings, for the *ka* of Usertesen II, now in the Gizeh Museum. Strange to say, there is not a trace of a coffin, or a lid to the sarcophagus; and, indeed, as this chamber is not under the middle of the pyramid, it may be questioned whether the real interment is not yet to be reached by some other passage.

From the north wall of this chamber a strange passage is cut in the rock, first northwards, then west, then south, then east, and lastly northwards again, opening into the limestone chamber ; in fact, it passes around the granite chamber. It was not a workman's passage intended to be closed up again, as the doorway of it has a bevelled edge and is curved at the top. It rather looks as if intended to prove to any spoilers that there was no other concealed passage leading out from the granite chamber, and thus to check their destructive searchings. If so, we may be tolerably certain that there is some other chamber containing the real interment.

The chambers in the pyramid are to the east of the centre; and adjoining the east face of the pyramid externally there stood a shrine, on the walls of which were figured the tables and lists of offerings for the *ka* of Usertesen II. The sculptures were of beautiful work, and brilliantly coloured. What process was used for fixing these coats of colour we do not know ; but still, from over four thousand years, after being broken and thrown into heaps, these colours are firmly fixed on the stone, and soaking and washing make no change in them. Only one large piece was found, now in the Gizeh Museum, but hundreds of portions of hieroglyphs were recovered among the chips. Who the destroyers were we can guess by an inscription of Ramessu II, rudely painted on a block of the stone. Among the ruins some chips of a black-granite seated statue of Usertesen II, were found, showing that the shrine was furnished like the earlier temples of the fourth dynasty.

The regular temple of the pyramid stood about half a mile to the east of it, on the edge of the desert ; and it has been destroyed like the shrine, and by the same hands, as two cartouches of Ramessu II were found on the blocks; several beads, &c., of the nineteenth dynasty occur in the ruins; and I found the name of Usertesen II on a piece of a granite pillar of Ramessu II at Ahnas, some miles to the south, showing for what purpose Illahun had been plundered. The outline of the temple can be traced by the thick brick wall which surrounded it. The plan is square, and it seems to have consisted of brickwork externally, lined with limestone masonry. But of the internal arrangement not a trace can be recovered. Probably a shrine of granite stood at the west end of the court, and objects of sandstone in the area, judging by the position of the chips. Also a large basalt statue existed here, of which only one fragment was found; the statue must therefore have been removed (probably to Ahnas), and not broken up here. One interesting discovery was made, however. In the middle of the area I noticed a slight hollow in the rock surface, about two and a half feet square. I thought of a foundation deposit, and examined this place. A block of stone lay fitted into it; on breaking and raising this, a second block was seen; when that was removed, we found plain sand. Scraping this out, we came on much broken pottery, and then some bronze models of tools, and a large number of carnelian beads. There were four sets of objects, thrown in pell mell; but the strings of carnelian beads, all exactly alike, are a puzzle. Is it possible that they were bead-money? They have the requisites of an exchange standard, as well as gold; they need a regular amount of labour to produce them, they are unalterable, and they serve for ornament when not used for exchange. However that may be, we have here far the oldest foundation-deposit known.

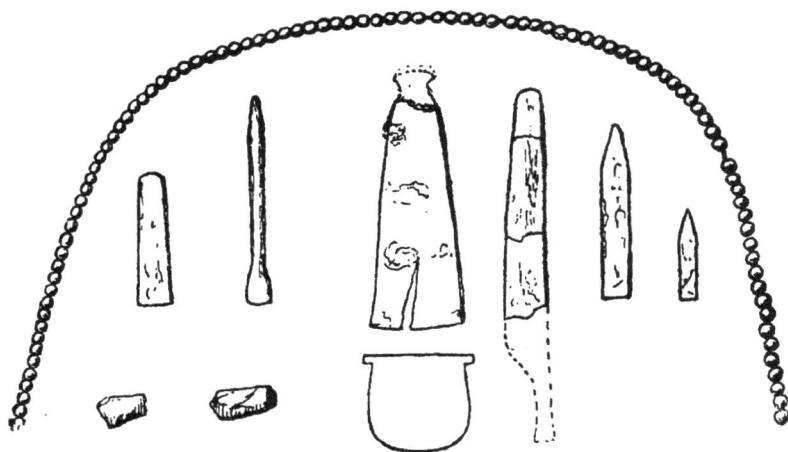

82. FOUNDATION DEPOSIT.   1 : 4.

The great prize of Illahun was unknown and unsuspected by anyone. On the desert adjoining the north side of the temple, I saw evident traces of a town, brick walls, houses and pottery ; moreover, the pottery was of a style as yet unknown to me. The town-wall started out in a line with the face of the temple ; and it dawned on me that this could hardly be other than the town of the pyramid builders, originally called Ha-Usertesen-hotep, and now known as Kahun. A little digging soon put it beyond doubt, as we found cylinders of that age, and no other; so that it was evident that I actually had in hand an unaltered town of the twelfth dynasty, regularly laid out by the royal architect for the workmen and stores, required in building the pyramid and its temple. After a few holes had been made, I formed up the workmen in a line along the outermost street, and regularly cleared the first line of chambers, turning the stuff into the street; then the chambers beyond those were emptied into them; and so line after line, block after block, almost every room in the town was

83. NORTH SIDE OF KAHUN, SHOWING LINE OF TOWN WALL.

emptied out and searched. The only part not quite cleared was where habitations had been formed in Roman times by lime-burners, who had disturbed the place and destroyed the ancient walls. Every chamber as it was cleared was measured and planned, and we can see the exact scheme of the architect, and where he expanded the town as time went on.

The general outline was a square mass; walled on

the west, north, and east sides, but open on the south
to the Nile plain, and not fully built out in this
direction.   In this space were buildings adjoining the
wall all round; within them a main street around
three sides of a square block of buildings in the
middle; and minor streets subdividing the buildings.
Then outside the wall on the west the town was

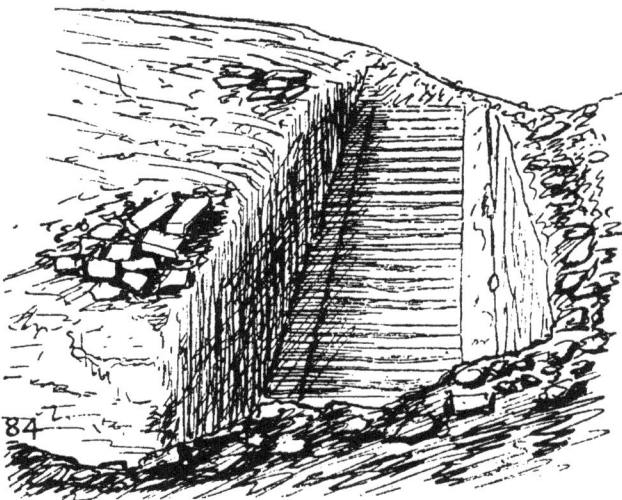

84. STEPS TO UPPER BUILDINGS ON HILL.

enlarged by a further space, also walled, and divided
by a long main street, and cross streets all the way
along it.   The larger houses all have a court, or
atrium, with columns around the middle of it, and in
the centre a small stone tank let into the ground
with a square of limestone around it five feet each
way.   These columns were sometimes of stone, sometimes of wood; with a simple abacus, or with a carved
palm capital; octagonal, or fluted, or ribbed: but

they always had large circular stone bases, which mostly remain in place in the rooms. The roofing was usually of beams, overlaid with bundles of straw, and mud-plastered; but many arched roofs of brickwork remain, some entire, others with only the lower part. The doorways were always arched in brickwork, and we know now for certain that the arch

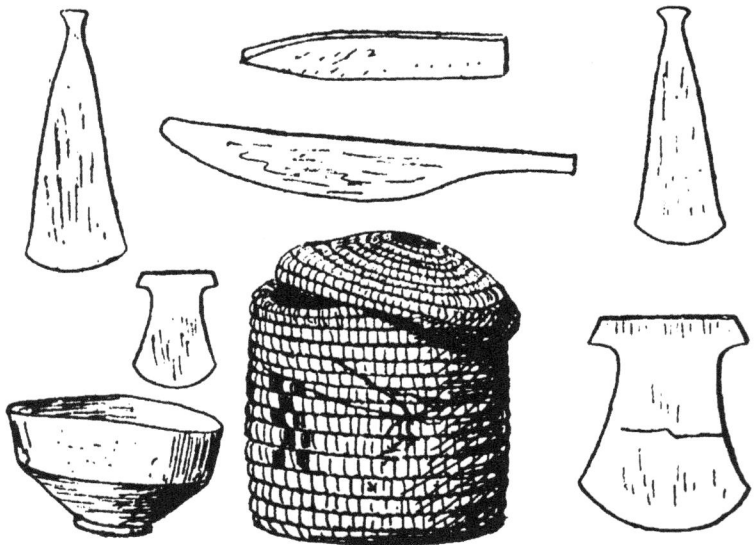

85. BASKET WITH TOOLS. 1:7.

was not only known, but was in constant use by the early Egyptians.

In the rooms pottery was often found; and many parts of the town having been deserted when the building of the pyramid was finished, the empty rooms were used as rubbish holes by the inhabitants who remained; in such places there might be even six or eight feet depth of broken pottery, woodwork and other things. Tools

were also found hidden in the dust which had lain in
the chambers; and one basket was found with a lid,
marvellously fresh and firm, containing copper hatchets
and chisels, and a copper bowl, all as free from rust as
when they were buried.   Beneath the brick floors of
the rooms was, however, the best place to search; not
only for hidden things, such as a statuette of a dancer

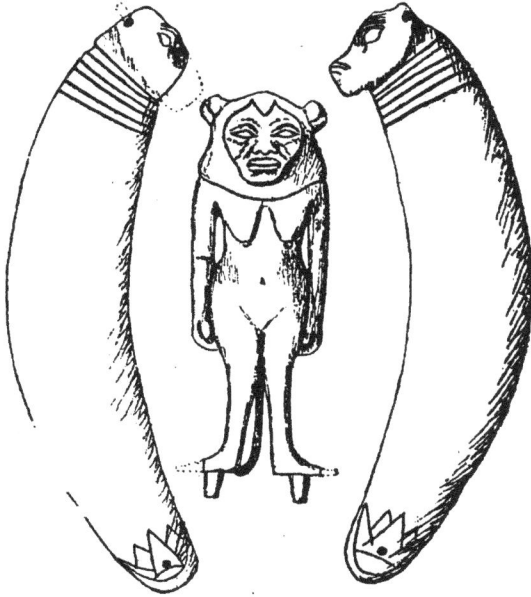

86. CASTANETS AND FIGURE OF DANCER.

and pair of ivory castanets, but also for numerous
burials of babies in wooden boxes.   These boxes had
been made for clothes and household use, but were
used to bury infants, often accompanied by necklaces
and other things.   On the necklaces were sometimes
cylinders with the kings' names; and thus we know for

certain that these burials, and the inhabitation of the town, is of the twelfth dynasty, from Usertesen II onward. Lying on one box was a splendid ivory carving of a baboon seated, of the most naturalistic work, comparable with the best cinquecento Italian ivories. This of course is kept at the Gizeh Museum. In the houses but little sculpture was found ; far the finest piece being a basalt statute of an official, now also at the Gizeh Museum.

The domestic remains were of great interest ; beside the pottery there were balls of thread, linen cloth, knives and tools of copper and of flint, a mirror of copper (Group 92), fishing nets, and many wooden tools, hoes, rakes, a brick-mould, plasterers' floats, mallets, copper chisels set in wooden handles, &c. Also games (Group 93) as whip-tops, tip-cats, draught-boards, dolls, and a beautifully woven sling. Many pieces of furniture were found, among them the greater part of a finely-made slender chair of dark wood inlaid with ivory pegs. Blue-glazed pottery

87. IVORY BABOON.

was not unusual, several figures of animals and pieces of bowls being found. Hitherto we had never known how the Egyptians obtained fire, as there is no sign of this on the sculptures, nor do they seem to have

attached any significance to fire-making. In this town
I found several sticks with the burnt holes made by

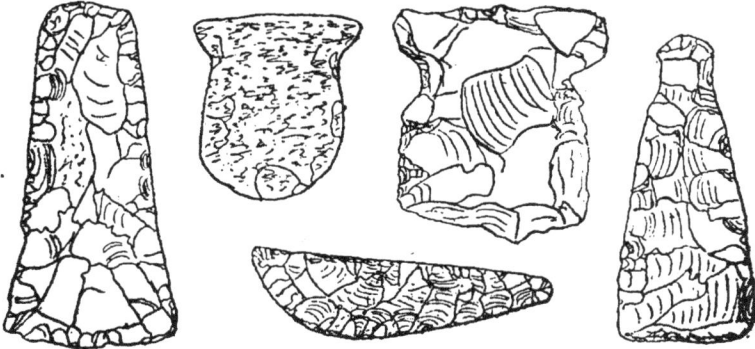

88. FLINT TOOLS. 1 : 6

drilling fire, as many races do at present : the
Egyptians probably did this with the bow-drill, with

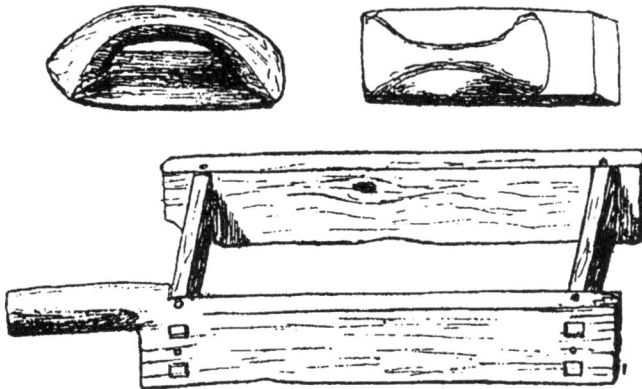

89. PLASTERERS' FLOATS, AND BRICK-MOULD.

which they were so familiar, and of which specimens
were found here.

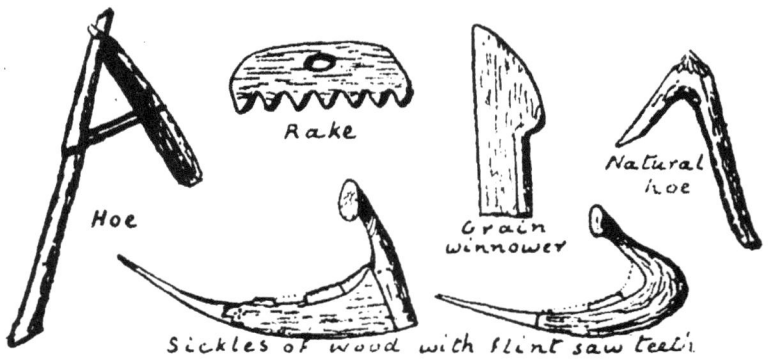

Hoe

Rake

Grain
winnower

Natural
hoe

Sickles of wood with flint saw teeth

90. AGRICULTURAL TOOLS OF WOOD. 1 : 20.

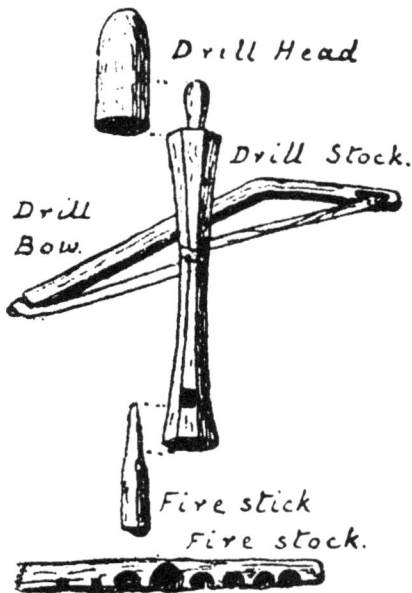

Drill Head

Drill Stock.

Drill
Bow.

Fire stick
Fire stock.

91. FIRE APPARATUS. 1 : 10.

Not only do we in this town drop into the midst of
the daily life and productions of this early age, but
the documents of the time also remain.   In various
chambers papyri were found; some carefully sealed
up and put by, such as the wills of Uah, and Antef-

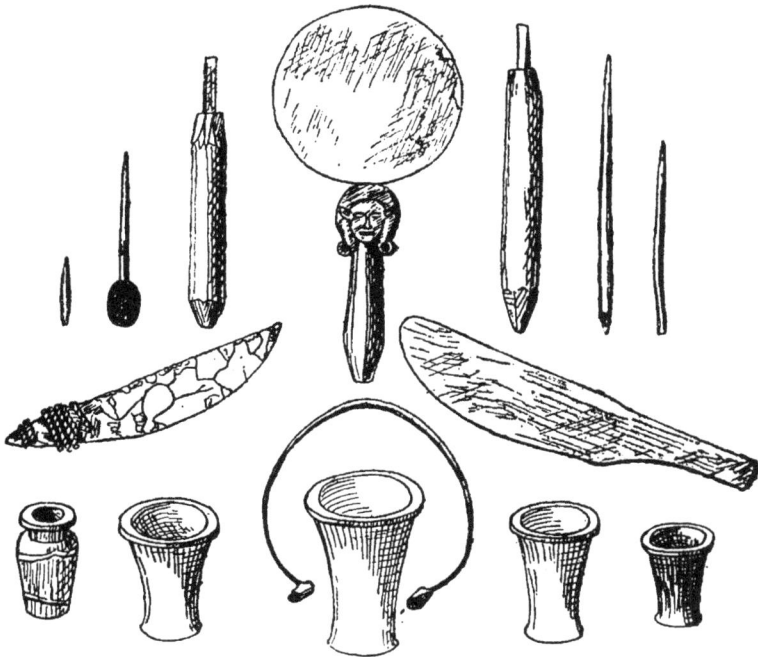

92 SET OF TOOLS, VASES, AND MIRROR.   1 : 8.

meri, but mostly thrown aside as waste paper.   One
of the largest is a hymn of praise to Usertesen III;
some pages of a medical work, some of a veterinary
papyrus, and innumerable parts of letters, accounts,
and memoranda make up the collection.   As only
five papyri of this early date were known before now,
this is a wide addition to our resources.

Another subject has quite unexpectedly come to light. Marks of various kinds are found on pieces of pottery-vessels here; some put·on by the maker before the baking, but mostly scratched by the owner. These marks are many of them derived from the Egyptian workmen's signs, corruptions of hieroglyphics. But, as we shall see in the next chapter, the discoveries at Guroh point to these having some kinship with the Western alphabets. They are therefore the venerable

93. CLAY TOYS, TWELFTH DYNASTY.

first step in adopting marks to represent sounds, irrespective of their primitive form and significance.

That these marks were known not only to Egyptians, but to foreigners here as well, is probable from the discoveries of Aegean pottery in this place. Intermixed with, and even beneath, the rubbish mounds of the twelfth dynasty are pieces of pottery which appear to be the forerunners of what we know as Greek pottery in later ages. The ware, the motives of the decoration, belong to the Aegean, and not to Egypt; either Greece or Asia Minor was their home, but long centuries before any specimens that we yet know of from those countries. The weights found here also testify to foreign influences, the greater part of them being on the Phoenician, Aeginetan, and Hittite standards.

Some later times have left their traces in this place, although the bulk of it is purely of the twelfth dynasty. A wooden stamp of Apepi was found, probably of the Hyksos king ; and if so, the only small article yet known of that dynasty. A small papyrus of Amenhotep III was found, rolled up, and placed in a pottery cylinder : also a splendid 'hunting scarab' of that king, recording his slaying 102 lions, which is of brilliant and perfect blue-green glaze. A broken papyrus of Amenhotep IV was also left here. But the main prize was a family tomb, probably of the end of the nineteenth, or early twentieth, dynasty. A cellar cut in the rock, belonging to one of the houses of the twelfth dynasty, had been found at this later date, and used as a sepulchre. More than a dozen coffins were piled in it, each containing several bodies, all the wrappings of which were reduced to black sooty dust. I stripped off the work, and for hours was occupied in opening coffin after coffin, carefully searching the dust inside each, cataloguing everything as I found it, overhauling the pottery and stone vases heaped in the chambers, and handing everything out to the one native lad whom I took down to help me. At last I finished the place, and came out much like a coal-heaver or a sweep, so that I had to go to the nearest pond to wash all over. Though none of the interments were rich, yet there were interesting

objects, and some foreign ; and above all we had the
whole find completely recorded, and the positions of
things noted exactly as they had b██ left by the
interrers. A curious point is that though the pottery,
and the decoration of one of the coffins, precludes our
dating this earlier than the end of the nineteenth

94., OBJECTS FROM MAKET TOMB. 1 : 10.

dynasty, yet all the scarabs on the bodies are of the
early part of the eighteenth dynasty, down to
Tahutmes III ; excepting a few of the twelfth dynasty,
doubtless found, as we found so many, in this town.
That all the decorations should be heirlooms is a
strange fact. In the richest coffin, the only one con-

taining a. name, that of the lady Maket, were two musical reeds, carefully slipped inside a larger reed for protection ; the scale shown by their holes is the major scale. The pottery here was remarkable; not only are there none of the styles characteristic of the eighteenth and nineteenth dynasties, so well known at Tel Amarna and Gurob, but the greater part is Phoenician, and not Egyptian, in its paste and its forms ; while among it is an Aegean vase, with an ivy leaf and stalk on each side, the earliest style of natural decoration after the period of geometrical. Some vases of green paste here are curious, one in the form of a horn stopped at the wide end.

Of later date still was a large wooden door, which had been probably brought from some other place in Roman times, and used here for a house. It had been made by Usarkon I ; and when the bronze head and foot-bands were incised with his name, the wood beneath had received the impression, which it retained after all the bronze had been removed. On the middle of the door there had been a scene of Usarkon offering to Neit and Horus, but this had been almost all chiselled away anciently. This door is now in the Gizeh Museum.

The next period of importance at Illahun is from the twenty-second to the twenty-fifth dynasties. The hills near the pyramid had been much used for rock tombs and mastabas of the pyramid period ; but these had been plundered and destroyed in early times, and the excavations were re-used during the later Bubastite and Ethiopian dynasties. These interments are generally rude, the coffins seldom having any intelligible inscription ; but mostly sham copies of the usual formula, put on by a decorator who could not read. The only fine tomb I found here was that of a priestess, Amenardus; her sarcophagus has carved inscriptions along the edges and down the corner-posts, and the coffin and that of her father are finely painted : these are now at Gizeh. Many of the mummies have bead net-works and patterns upon them, with figures of winged scarabs, the four genii, the *ba* bird, and other emblems, all executed in coloured beads. As the threading is completely rotted, the beads all fall apart with the slightest shake, and such work is therefore never preserved when excavations are left to the native overseers. When we entered a tomb, I opened the coffins in the gentlest way, drawing or cutting out the pegs which fastened them ; and then a glance inside showed if any bead-work existed. If there were bead patterns, the next step was to fetch a petroleum stove down into the chamber, melt a batch of beeswax, and then when it was on the point of chilling, ladle it out, and dash it over the bead-work. If the wax is too hot it sinks in, and soaks all the mummy wrappings into a solid mass; if poured on, it runs off the body in a narrow stream. When all the beads were covered, and the wax set, I then lifted up the sheet of wax with the bead-work sticking to it, flattened it out on a board, and it was ready for fixing in a tray permanently, with the lower side turned outward.

The amulets found in these tombs are all of the figures of deities, specially Bast, and are of pottery covered with light olivey-green glazes, quite different from those of the nineteenth or twentieth dynasties. A revival of glazed work took place under the twenty-second dynasty, of very delicate character, and fine glazing. But the amulet system went into a very different stage in the twenty-sixth dynasty; then in place of two or three, generally varying in size, we find dozens all uniform in style, either of pottery or of polished stone, arranged in rows on the mummy according to a system. Such was the plan of the amulets at Hawara and at Nebesheh.

Yet a later period had left its remains at Illahun. In Coptic times, about the sixth and seventh century A.D., the ground all about the temple, and on a hill near the canal, was used for a cemetery. Though I could not spend time on clearing such remains myself, the people of the place readily grubbed up their forefathers, and disposed of their garments to anyone who would buy them. I thus obtained a large quantity of embroideries and woven stuffs, the best of which are now at South Kensington.

Illahun has then proved of great value to our knowledge of Egyptian civilization; it has shown us a completely arranged town of the middle kingdom; it has surrounded us with all the products and manufactures of that age; it reveals the simultaneous use of finely wrought flint tools with those of copper, when bronze was yet unknown; it provides us with the writings of the period, including a will two thousand years older than any known before; the pyramid proves to be of a design new to us, and contains one of the finest examples of mechanical skill; while of later ages we learn the date of Phoenician pottery, and of the earliest figured Greek vases, and can trace the history of the use of amulets. Of the blanks in the history of civilization, one more has been filled up.

95. FLINT HIPPOPOTAMUS, TWELFTH DYNASTY.

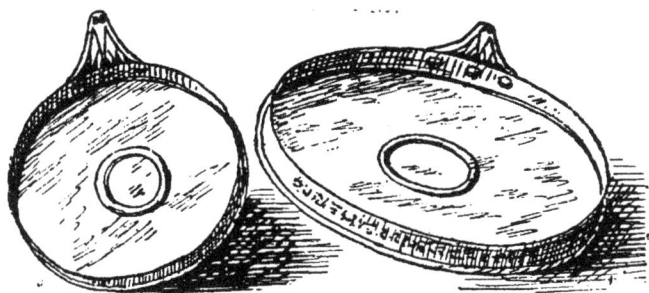

96. Bronze Pans, Nineteenth Dynasty.

CHAPTER IX.

GUROB.

1889–90.

At the mouth of the Fayum, on the opposite side to Illahun, stood in later times another town, founded by Tahutmes III, and ruined under Merenptah; thus its history falls within about two-and-a-half centuries. While I was working at Hawara some beads and ornaments were brought to me from this place; I soon went to see it, and found that it was an early site un-mixed with any later remains. In the beginning of 1889 I worked out part of the town, and the rest of it was cleared by Mr. Hughes-Hughes in the end of that year, while I worked at Illahun. The general arrange-ment of it was a large walled enclosure, within which were two other enclosures side by side, one containing the temple, the other a small town. The temple had been founded by Tahutmes III, and had lasted through Khuenaten's changes only to be destroyed soon after, probably by Ramessu II, when he carried away the temples of Illahun. That the town was ruined early in the reign of Merenptah is indicated by the sudden end of the previous abundance of scarabs and rings with the kings' names at this point ; of later times only one or two objects of Ramessu III have been found.

Of purely Egyptian objects many were discovered, but the main interest of the place is in the remains of foreigners from

97. BRONZE INTERLOCKING HINGES.

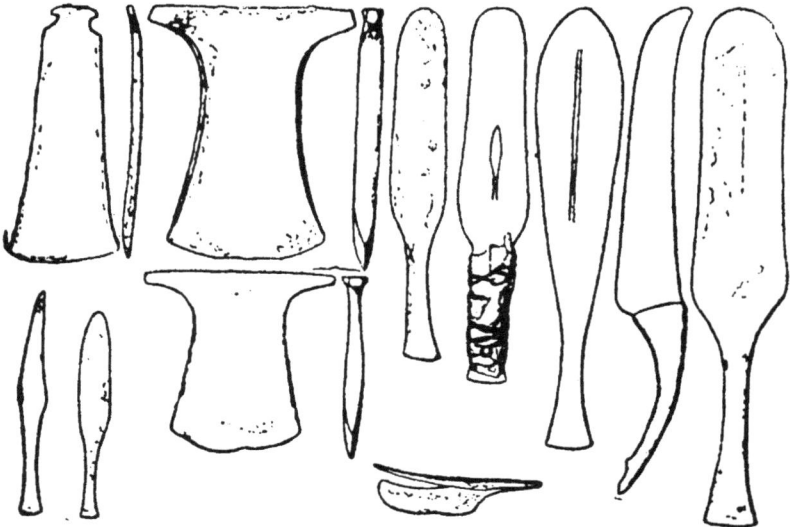

98. BRONZE TOOLS. 1 : 6.

the Mediterranean who lived here. Of Egyptian work

K

we may mention two funeral tablets (one now at Gizeh);
a lion's head, probably the terminal to the side of a
staircase ; two splendid bronze pans (Group 96), still
bright and fresh and elastic, most skilfully wrought
(now at Gizeh) ; a beautiful wooden statuette of a lady
named Res, clad in the ribbed drapery of the Rames_
side age (also at Gizeh) ; a statuette of a priestess,

99. COFFIN HEAD OF ANEN THE TURSHA OFFICIAL. 1 : 16.

and a figure of a girl swimming holding a duck, carved
in wood (at Gizeh); a wooden box for papyri, inscribed (at Gizeh) ; and some necklaces found in the
town. Some bronze hinges, hatchets, chisels, and
knives were also found, one by one, in different rooms.
    The foreign inhabitants, although conforming to
Egyptian ways in some respects, have left many

100. WOODEN STATUETTES OF A PRIESTESS, AND THE LADY RES.

traces here.   Foremost is the coffin of a high official
who was of the Tursha race, the
Turseni, probably, of the northern
Aegean.   The ushabti figure of a
Hittite, Sadi-amia, was found in
an adjoining grave.   A wooden
figure of a Hittite harper, wearing
the great pigtail of his race, was
picked up in the town.   A bronze

101. HITTITE HARPER. mirror, with a Phoenician Venus
holding a dove as the handle of it, was found in a
tomb.   While constantly
Aegean vases, such as
those of the first period
of Mykenae, are found in
both the town and in
tombs.   The Greek cus-
tom of a funereal pyre
remained here in a modi-
fied form ; although the
body appears to have
been buried in Egyptian
fashion (as I found light
hair on some of the mum-
mies here), yet the personal
articles were all burnt.
Apparently on the death
of the owner a hole was
dug in the floor of the
room ;   into   this   were

102. PHOENICIAN VENUS MIRROR. placed the chair, the clothing, the mirror, combs, necklaces and toilet articles, the

glass bottles, the blue-glazed bowls and vases, the alabaster dishes, the knife and other implements, and the best pottery of the deceased.

All these were burnt; the fire was smothered with potsherds laid over it; earth was then filled in, and the brick

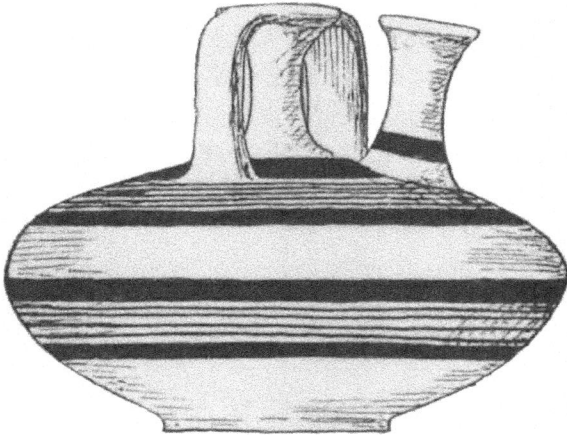

103. AEGEAN VASES.   1 : 2.

104. BLUE AND YELLOW GLASS BOTTLE.

floor of the room was relaid. No such custom is ever known among Egyptians, and this shows again the foreign occupation of the place. We know from in-scriptions how the Mediterranean races, Libyans,

Akhaians, Turseni, and others had pushed into Egypt
from the west, and that they had settled in the Nile
valley to even somewhat south of the Fayum.   This
place was evidently then one of their settlements, and
its sudden fall under Merenptah just agrees to his
expulsion of all these foreigners in the fifth year of

105. BLUE-GLAZED VASES. 1 : 6.

his reign.   We have here then before our eyes the
remains of that great invasion which has always
hitherto been a literary shadow without material
substance.

As before mentioned, the marks on pottery so often
found in the town of the twelfth dynasty at Illahun, are
also found at Gurob.   The list of signs used is somewhat different, but the greater part may be identified ;
and it is impossible to deny that they are the same
as a whole, though naturally modified by alteration,
addition, and omission, in the course of a thousand
years.   Having now, therefore, this body of signs in
use in 1200 B. C. in a town occupied by people of the
Aegean and Asia Minor, Turseni, Akhaians, Hittites,
and others, it will require a very certain proof of the

supposed Arabian source of the Phoenician alphabet, before we can venture to deny that we have here the origin of the Mediterranean alphabets.

106. BLUE-GLAZED BOWLS.

Besides these remains, Gurob proved to be a treasury of a later age. In the Ptolemaic period some town had existed in this neighbourhood, the inhabitants of which were buried here in the edge of the desert, apart from the earlier town. Their mummies are destitute of amulets or ornaments, and have all gone to black dust, their cartonnage coverings are without names, and of the most conventional and uninteresting kind, and their coffins are of prodigious rudeness, worthy of a savage of the Pacific ; while their tombs are rude holes scooped in the sandy soil. In no respect would these burials seem worth notice, had not the cartonnage makers used up old papyri as the cheapest material for their trade. But what was worthless in the days of Philadelphos is a treasure now ; the soldiers' wills appointing as executors the sovereigns, Philadelphos and Arsinoe, the private letters, the leaves of Plato and unknown Greek plays, the accounts,—all these can be unfolded from what looks like hopeless rubbish. The cartonnage in the earlier examples was glued together, and this has not only injured the writing, but almost always served as a bait to worms, who have destroyed it ; but later on the makers found that simple wetting and moulding would suffice, and we can now often peel apart sheet after sheet of writing as fresh as in the days when Cleopatra was yet unborn.

Some remains of even later times are found here ; and I obtained from native diggers many Coptic embroideries, and a beautiful set of Roman glass vessels.

The essential value of Gurob is in giving us a thoroughly fixed date for the earlier stages of the civilization of Greece ; in showing the races of the

Mediterranean [at home in Egypt; and in explaining how far they had imbibed Egyptian culture during their first sojourn on the Nile; and what they may be expected to have borrowed from thence at this early period.

107. IVORY DUCK BOX.   1 : 2.

108. Pyramid of Medum.

CHAPTER X.

MEDUM.

1891.

AFTER having sampled the civilization of each of the great periods of Egyptian history, back to the twelfth dynasty, as described in preceding chapters, I longed more than ever to discover the beginning of things. For this Medum offered the best chance for reaching back. The presumption was that it belonged to the beginning of the fourth dynasty; and here we might perhaps find something still undeveloped, and be able to gauge our way in the unknown. Could we there see the incipient stages, or at least their traces? Could we learn how conventional forms and ideas had arisen? Could we find Egypt not yet full grown, still in its childhood?

I called together a selected lot of my old workers

from Illahun, and we went over and made a camp at the cemetery of Medum ; there we lived over four months, and I unravelled what could be traced on the questions that await us. Broadly, it may be said, that we learned more of our ignorance than our knowledge : the beginning seems as remote as ever, for nearly all the conventions are already perfected there; but many new questions have been opened, and we at least see more of the road, though the goal is still out of view.

The first question to settle was that of the age of the pyramid and cemetery. All the indications pointed to as early an age as we knew, but not before Seneferu, the first king of the fourth dynasty, and predecessor of Khufu. Yet the theory that the pyramids were built in chronological order, from north to south, had led some to suppose that this was of the twelfth dynasty.

The most promising means of ascertaining the age, was to search for any remains of the pyramid temple ; on the chance of inscriptions, such as I had found of Khafra at Gizeh, and of Usertesen II at Illahun. But where was the temple? No sign of such a building could be seen anywhere to the east of the pyramid, and some holes I sunk in the space within the pyramid enclosure showed nothing. I hesitated for some days, while other work was going on, looking at the great bank of rubbish against the side of the pyramid, rubbish accumulated by the destruction of its upper part. At last I determined on the large excavation needful, for I felt that we must solve the matter if possible. So, marking out a space which would have held two or three good-sized London houses, and knowing that we must go as deep as a tall house before we could get any result, I began a work of several weeks, with as many men as could be efficiently put into the area. At first it was easy enough, but soon we found large blocks, which we could scarcely move; and these slipped away and rolled down all the stages of our work, upsetting all our regular cutting. But they all had to be got out of the way, by lifting, rolling or breaking up. At last we had a hole that could be seen for miles off across the valley, and so deep that the sides looked perilously high on either hand when one stood in the bottom. The pavement was reached, and we found at one end of our great excavation a wall, and one side of a large stele just showing.

We needed then to lengthen the pit, and the falls from our fresh work soon buried all that we had found. A fresh trouble came with a strong gale, which blew away the sand, and let the loose stones come rattling down from the rubbish which formed the sides of our hole. One great fall came near burying us in the bottom of the work : and it was three weeks before I again saw the building. At last we uncovered the court-yard, and found two steles ; and moreover instead of a mere court there appeared a doorway on the east side, and crawling in I found a chamber and passage still roofed over and quite perfect. We had, in fact, found an absolutely complete, though small, temple ; not a stone was missing, nor a piece knocked off ; the steles and the altar between them stood just as when they were set up ; and the oldest dated building in the land has stood unimpaired amidst all the building and the destruction that has gone on in Egypt throughout history.

The question about the age was settled indirectly. The original construction had no ornament or inscriptions. But numerous mentions of Seneferu, both during the ages near his own, and of the eighteenth dynasty, showed plainly what the Egyptians knew about the builder.

109. COURT OF TEMPLE.

The pyramid of Medum differs from nearly all the others. It is really the primitive tomb-building or mastaba, such as often is found with successive coats added around it in the cemetery here ; but this was enlarged by seven coats of masonry, widening and heightening it, until a final coat over all covered the slope from top to bottom at one angle. It is thus the final stage of complication of the mastaba tomb, and the first type of the pyramid. Later kings saved the intermediate stages, and built pyramids all at one design, without any additions. This architectural feature is another proof of the early age of this pyramid. And it is remarkably akin to the pyramid of Khufu which follows it. Both have the same angle ; and therefore the ratio of height to circuit, being that of a radius to its circle, holds good. The approximate ratio adopted was 7 to 44 ; the dimensions of the pyramid of Seneferu are 7 and 44 times a length of 25 cubits ; those of Khufu are 7 and 44 times a length of 40 cubits. Hence the design of the size of

110. SECTION OF PYRAMID. 1 : 2000.

the great pyramid of Gizeh was made by Khufu on the lines of the pyramid of Medum, which was built by his predecessor. Fragments of Seneferu's wooden coffin were found inside the pyramid ; but the place had long since been plundered.

The tombs at Medum proved of great interest.

One of the largest was built on a very irregular foundation ; and below the ground level I found the walls by which the builders had guided their work. Outside of each corner a wall was built up to the ground level ; the sloping profile of the side was drawn on it ; and then the wall was founded and built in line between the profiles. But the most attractive matter was the study of the inscriptions on the tombs, which show us the earliest forms of the hieroglyphs yet

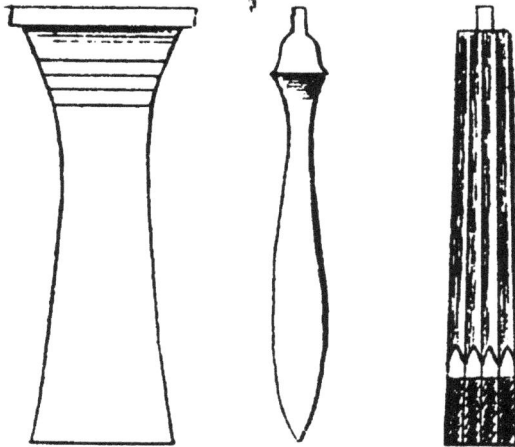

111. COLUMNS OF THIRD DYNASTY.

known. To preserve and examine their record I made a full-sized copy of the whole, and then published that reduced by photo-lithography. The evidence is the most valuable that we can yet obtain, on the earliest traceable civilization of the Egyptians. We have no remains certainly dated older than these ; and the objects used as hieroglyphs here must have been already long familiar for them to have been used for signs. They therefore lead us back to the third dynasty, or even earlier times; and they show us various objects which are as yet quite unknown to us till much later ages.

We can thus estimate the architecture of the pre-pyramid period. There were columns with spreading capitals and abaci, set up in rows to support the roof. There were papyrus columns, with a curious bell-top on the flower, the source of the heavier conventional form of later times; these were probably carved in wood, and originated from a wooden tent pole. There were octagonal fluted columns tapering to the top, and painted with a black dado, a white ornamental band, and red above. There was the cornice of uraeus serpents, which is so ·familiar in later times. And the granaries were already built with sloping sides, as seen on later tombs. In short, all the essentials of an advanced architecture seem to have been quite familiar to the Egyptians; and we must cease to argue from the simplicity of the religious buildings which we know—such as the granite temples of Gizeh, or the limestone temple of Medum—for deciding on the architecture of the fourth and third dynasties. We seem to be as far from a real beginning as ever.

The animals drawn here show that the domestica-tion of various species was no uncommon thing; apes, monkeys, many kinds of horned cattle, ibexes, &c., and various birds, all appear familiarly in this age. And of the wild birds the eagle, owl, and wag-tail, are admirably figured, far better than in later times. The Libyan race was already a civilized ally of Egypt, using bows and arrows much as we see them subsequently. The tools employed were of the established types; the adze and the chisel of bronze; the sickle of flint teeth set in wood; the axe of stone; the head of the bow drill—all these are shown us. And the exactitude of the standards of measure was a matter of careful concern; the cubit here does not differ from the standard of later times more than the thickness of a bit of stout card. The draught-board was exactly the same as that which is found down to Greek times.

Some matters, however, point to a stage which passed away soon after. The sign for a seal is not a scarab, or a ring, but a cylinder of jasper, set in gold ends, and turning on a pin attached to a necklace of stone beads. Cylinders are often met with in early times, but died out of use almost entirely by the eighteenth dynasty. This points to a connection with Babylonia in early times. The numerals are all derived from various lengths of rope; pointing to an original reckoning on knotted ropes, as in many other countries. And some suggestion of the original home of Egyptian culture near the sea, is made by the signs for water being all black or dark blue-green. This is a colour that no one living on the muddy Nile would ever associate with water; rather should we suppose it to have originated from the clear waters of the Red Sea.

Another glimpse of the prehistoric age in Egypt is afforded by the burials at Medum. The later people always buried at full length, and with some provision for the body, such as food, head-rests, &c. Such

burials are found among the nobles at Medum. But
most of the people there buried in a contracted form,
nose and knees, or at least with the thigh bent square
with the body and heels drawn up. And moreover,
no food-vessels or other objects are put in. Yet
there was no mere indifference shown ; the bodies are
in deep well tombs, often placed in large wooden
boxes, which must have been valuable in Egypt, and
always lying with the head to the north, facing the
east. Here is clearly a total difference in beliefs, and
probably also in race. We know that two races, the
aquiline-nosed and the snouty, can be distinguished
in early times ; and it seems that the aborigines used
the contracted burial, and the dynastic race the
extended burial, which—with its customs—soon became the national mode.

Is it likely that the bulk of the people should have
resisted this change for some 800 years, and then have
suddenly adopted it in two or three generations?
Does not this rapid adoption of the upper-class custom, between the beginning of the fourth dynasty and
the immediately succeeding times, suggest that the
dynastic race did not enter Egypt till shortly before
we find their monuments? At least, the notion that
the stages preceding the known monuments should
be sought outside of Egypt, and that this is the ex-
planation of the dearth of objects before the fourth
dynasty, is strengthened by the change of custom and
belief which we then find.

The mutilations and diseases that come to light are
remarkable. One man had lost his left leg below the
knee ; another had his hand cut off and put in the

tomb; others seem to have had bones excised, and placed separately with the body. In one case acute and chronic inflammation and rheumatism of the back had united most of the vertebrae into a solid mass down the inner side. In another case there had been a rickety curvature of the spine. To find so many peculiarities in only about fifteen skeletons which I collected, is strange. These are all in the Royal College of Surgeons now, for study.

Medum has, then, led us some way further back than we had reached before in the history of Egyptian civilization; but it has shown how vastly our information must be increased before the problems are solved.

CHAPTER XI.

THE FRESH LIGHT ON THE PAST.

IT might seem as if the researches described in these chapters were, though interesting in themselves, yet not of particular account in the wider view of human history and civilization. It is to focus together this new information, to show the results which flow from it, and to give a connected idea of our fresh light on the past, that this chapter is placed here. The application of scientific principles to archaeology, the opening of fresh methods of enquiry, and the rigorous notice of the period of everything found, have been as fruitful in the East as it has proved to be in the West.

In Egypt, the oldest condition of the present country that is known—the beginning of history as distinct from geology—is an age of great rainfall and denudation ; succeeding to the geological age, in which the existing masses of surface gravels were laid down. This rain nourished a dense vegetation, of which the chance remains may be seen in the various silicified forests, which occur where circumstances favoured their preservation. The amount of water falling on the country swelled the volume of

the Nile to far beyond its greatest modern extent.
Between the cliffs on either hand it ran certainly
hundreds of feet higher than at present, probably in
part as an estuary. The cliffs all along the Nile are
worn by water running at a great height ; and the
débris brought down from the side valleys is piled
up in hills at the mouths of the valleys, in a way
that could only occur where they discharged into
deep water. That the rain sufficed to fill up such
a vast volume, we can believe, when we see the gorges
cut back in the sides of the Nile cliffs by the lateral
drainage. These often run back for some miles,
ploughed out by receding waterfalls—small Niagaras
—which have each left at the valley head their pre-
cipitous fall of polished rock, with a great basin below
it hollowed by the force of the torrent. Such was the
source of the power which has scoured out the whole
Nile valley for a depth of over two hundred feet.
High up on the hills between the Nile and the
Fayum, the very crest of the hill is entirely of gravels
and boulders, which can only have been deposited
when there was a dead level at that height across the
Nile valley. All the depths of the Nile below those
hills have been scoured out by the rainfall and the
torrent of the stream, some miles in width, and probably one to two hundred feet in depth. And the age
of this is not merely geological and beyond human
interests. Man was there at this time, as his rude
flint implement, river-worn and rolled, high upon the
hills, now shows us. (See Chap. VI. Fig. 58.)

We come down an age later. The Nile had fallen
to near its present level, but still filled its whole bed

to perhaps fifty feet deep. Vegetation still grew on the hills; for we find traces of man at this time, and he must have lived on something. Where he lived we can guess by the flints which he fashioned, and which the heavy rains swept away down the valleys, and bedded in the shoals of *débris* in the reduced and shallow river. These flints are now to be picked out from the sides of later cuttings which the rain has made through its old river deposits, now high and dry in air; and it is at the mouth of the valley of the tombs of the kings at Thebes that these flints have been collected.

After that, we know nothing more of man until we find that the country was in its present state,—without any rainfall for practical purposes, the hills all barren desert, the Nile only filling the bottom of its old bed for a few months of the year, and meandering the rest of the time in a channel cut in its own mud, and man cultivating the old bed of the river when it is not over-flowed. The civilization that we find before us in the earliest known history appears elaborate and perfect. After that, only slow changes of fashion and taste influenced it, and but few discoveries of importance were made during thousands of years which ensued. That this civilization was imported by an incoming race seems most probable; and the dynastic Egyptians found already in the country an aboriginal population, whose features, whose beliefs, and whose customs, differed much from their own. The two races had not yet amalgamated when we first come into their presence at Medum; but soon after that all signs of difference cease.

This earliest civilization was completely master of the arts of combined labour, of masonry, of sculpture, of metal-working, of turning, of carpentry, of pottery, of weaving, of dyeing, and other elements of a highly organized social life. And in some respects their work is quite the equal of any that has been done by mankind in later ages. Though simple, it is of extreme ability; and it is only in resources, and not in skill, that it has ever been surpassed. Certain products were then scarcely if at all known, and it is in the application of these that the civilization of later times shows a difference. No metal was used except copper, and hence flint was largely needed. And glass was probably unknown, although glazes were in use. But in most other respects the changes of later times are rather due to economy of production, and an increased demand for cheap imitations.

The work of the great period of the twelfth dynasty differs mainly in the freer use of writing, the greater quantity and poorer quality of the sculptures or paintings, and the introduction of glass and of glassy frits for colouring.

The next great period, the eighteenth to the nineteenth dynasty, is marked by the use of bronze, and the disappearance of flint tools. The art of glazing was much developed, and attained a brilliancy and variety of colouring, and a boldness of design, which was never again reached, unless perhaps by the mediaeval Orientals. But artistically the finest work of this age scarcely reaches the perfection of the sculpture and drawing which had already passed away.

The next serious change was the introduction of

iron, of which there is no satisfactory evidence until about 800 B.C. Iron may have been known perhaps as a curiosity, just as one example of bronze occurs two thousand years before it came into actual use; but it had no effect on the arts. And shortly after came the Egyptian renascence, when the cycle of invention was run through, and the Egyptians were reduced to copying slavishly, and without the original spirit, the works of their ancestors. The Western influence became predominant, and importations instead of development govern the succeeding changes.

But it is rather in Europe than in Egypt that our interest centres. As no European literature remains to us older than the sixth or seventh century B.C. (except the oral poems), it has been too readily assumed that no civilization worthy of the name could have dwelt here, and that we are indebted to the East for all our skill. So far from this being the case, it now seems that we must almost reverse the view. We have in the Egyptian records the accounts of a great European confederacy, which smote Egypt again and again,—Greece, Asia Minor, Italy, and Libya, all leagued together. We now know, from the objects found in Egypt, that these peoples were dwelling there as settlers so far back as 1400 B.C., if not indeed before 2000 B.C. From the chronology of the arts now ascertained, we can date the great civilization of Mykenae to about 1600 to 1000 B.C. (as I have stated in 'Notes on Mykenae,' *Journal of Hellenic Studies*, 1891); and we begin to see a great past rising before us, dumb, but full of meaning. Some of the metals were known in Europe before they appear in use in Egypt : the use of bronze is quite as old in the north as on the south of the Mediterranean ; and the tin of Egypt probably came from the mines of Hungary and Saxony, which most likely supplied Europe at that time. Iron appears in use in Europe as soon as in Egypt. The best forms of tools are known in Italy two or three centuries before Egypt possessed them.

What then may be concluded as to Europe, from our present point of view ? That Europe had an indigenous civilization, as independent of Egypt and Babylonia as was the indigenous Aryan civilization of India. That this civilization has acquired arts independently, just as much as India has, and that Europe has given to the East as much as it has borrowed from there. As early as 1600 B.C., it appears that a considerable civilization existed in Greece, which flourished in the succeeding centuries, especially in alliance with Libya. Probably it was already beginning in the period of the thirteenth dynasty, before 2000 B.C. By about 1400 B.C. a great proficiency in the arts is seen ; elaborate metal-work and inlaying was made, influenced by Egyptian design, but neither made in Egypt, nor by Egyptians. Glazed pottery painted with designs was successfully made, and the arts of glazing and firing were mastered. And by 1100 B.C. this civilization was already decadent. Moreover this was not only in a corner of Europe ; it had contact with the North as well as with Italy and Africa, and is at one with the culture of the bronze age, of which it is the crown and flower. Across Europe, from the Greek peninsula to the Baltic, this civilization stretches.

And though in Greece it ripened to an early fall, and was destroyed by the barbaric Dorian invasion, it retained its hardy power in the North and in Italy. When we come down to about 800 B.C., we find that the arts stood high in Northern Italy. The requirements of the carpenters and joiners of that age had led them to invent the most perfect forms of chisels ; and our mortising chisel and flat chisel with a tang have not received any improvement in the details of their form for 2700 years. The bronze age is the source of the objects we now use. Thence these types were carried into Egypt a couple of centuries later by the Greeks. When we descend further we see this independent culture of Europe prominent. The Saxons and Northmen did not borrow their weapons, their laws, or their thoughts from Greece or Italy. The Celts swamped the south of Europe at their pleasure ; and, against the fullest development of Greek military science, they were yet able to penetrate far south and plunder Delphi. They were powerful enough to raid Italy right across the Etrurian territory. When we look further east, we see the Dacians with weapons and ornaments and dresses which belong to their own civilization, and were not borrowed from Greece. In short, Greece and Italy did not civilise Europe ; they only headed the civilization for a brief period. And the Italian influence, which was much the more powerful, only lasted for a couple of centuries. From Caesar's campaigns to the end of the Antonines is the whole time of Italian supremacy. After that there never was a Roman emperor, excepting a few ephemeral reigns. The centre of power and authority in Europe was in the Balkan peninsula. The emperors were mainly natives of that region ; and the northern Holy Roman Empire of Germany has its roots practically in the third century. Civilization in Europe is, then, an independent growth, borrowing from, and lending to, the East. In the van of this group of races have come in turn Mykenaean Greece, then Etruria, Hellas, Rome, Dacia and Pannonia, the Lombards, and the Northmen ; and each in turn have impressed their character on those peoples who were less advanced. Our common belief in the overshadowing importance of Rome in all our history is probably largely influenced by our literary history being derived from Roman sources, and this Italian view being fed for ecclesiastical purposes in the Middle Ages. In the broader view of the history of civilization in Europe, the spread of law and Latin in Southern Europe is perhaps Rome's main result. But we must not forget that the Italian supremacy was quite as brief, if more potent, than that of other races who have led the way before and since.

We can now see somewhat of the wide results which have come to a great extent from the study of Egyptian civilization recorded in these pages, and the comparison of it with other countries. That vastly more remains to be worked out is painfully seen. We are only yet on the threshold of understanding the sources of the knowledge, the arts, and the culture, which we have inherited from a hundred generations.

CHAPTER XII.

THE ART OF EXCAVATING.

PROBABLY most people have somewhat the ideas of a worthy lady, who asked me how to begin to excavate a ruined town—should she begin to dig at the top or at the side? A cake or a raised pie was apparently in her mind, and the only question was where to best reach the inside of it. Now there are ruins and ruins : they may differ greatly in original nature, in the way they have been destroyed, and in the history of their degradation. The only rule that may be called general, is that digging must be systematic; chance trenches or holes seldom produce anything in themselves, they are but feelers. The main acquirement always needed is plenty of imagination. Imagination is the fire of discovery ; the best of servants, though the worst of masters. A habit of reasoning out the most likely cause, and all other possible causes, for the condition of things as seen, is essential. If there is a slope of the ground, a ridge, a hollow—Why is it there? What can have produced it? and Which cause is the most probable for it? The mere form of the ground will often show plainly what is beneath it. Is there a smooth uniform mound of large size ? Then a mass of house ruins of a town may be expected. Is

there a steep edge to it around ? Then there was a
wall, either of the town or of some one large building which forms the whole ruin. Is there a ring of
mounds with a central depression ? Then there was a
temple or large permanent building, with house ruins
around it. Is there a gentle slope up one side, and a

112. FORMS OF RUBBISH-HEAP, AND OF RUINS OF BUILDING.

sharp fall on the other ? Then it is a rubbish mound.
Is the mass high above the general soil ? Then several
successive layers of habitation may be expected.
So, even from afar, some ideas may be gleaned before
setting foot on a ruined site.

When we reach our town and walk over it, much
more can be seen of what is beneath. Very likely it
seems all irregular, hillocky, dusty ground, and who
can say what it may cover ? In one place, however,
we find that there are no chips or potsherds lying
about : track around, and find the space of this clearance, probably it runs along for some distance ; you
are on the top of a mud-brick wall, denuded down
to the level of the rubbish in which it is buried.
Follow the clear space, and you will outline the forti-
fications of the city or its temple. Or perhaps you
notice a difference in the vegetation—no plants will
grow on particular ground ; here is probably a mass of
hard mud-brick or stonework, without moisture or
nutriment, and you will thus find the walls. Or there
is a hollow or old pit met with ; here the modern
natives have been digging out stone masonry, and

around it, or below, may be the rest of a building. Some symmetrical form of the mounds can be detected, and we are perhaps led at once to the temple, or to trace out the streets of the town. Or a patch of ground is reddened with fire, showing that a house has been burnt there, and probably stone and metal and pottery may remain intact in the ruins. But our special notice must be given to the potsherds lying strewn all over the surface. Pottery is the very key to digging; to know the varieties of it, and the age of each, is the alphabet of work. Not that it is more distinctive in itself than most other products of various ages; but it is so vastly commoner than anything else, that a place may be dated in a minute by its pottery on the surface, which would require a month's digging in the inside of it to discover as much from inscriptions or sculptures. A survey showing the form of the ground, and the position of every fragment or indication that can be of use, is essential to understanding it; and will often point out, by the probable symmetry of parts, what are the best spots to examine first.

Having then made out as much as possible beforehand, we begin our diggings. If there appear to be remains of a temple, or some larger building, which should be thoroughly examined, we first make pits about one edge of the site, and find how far out the ruins extend. Having settled that, a large trench is dug along the whole of one side, reaching down to the undisturbed soil beneath, and about six or eight feet wide at the bottom, all the earth being heaped on the outer edge of the trench. Then the inner side is dug away, and the stuff thrown up on the outer side by a row of men all along the trench. Thus the trench is gradually swept across the whole site, always taking from one side, and throwing back on the other. Each block of stone or piece of building found is surveyed, and covered over again if not wanted ; sculptures or inscriptions are either removed or rolled up on to the surface of the stuff, or remain exposed in pits left in the rubbish. Thus the earth does not cover over and encumber the surrounding ground, which may very likely need to be excavated in its turn ; the stuff is removed a minimum distance, which means occupying a minimum of time and cost ; and the site is covered over again, to preserve from the weather and from plunderers any foundations or masonry that may remain. Every ounce of earth is thus examined, and all it contains is discovered. Town ruins may be treated in the same way ; all the chambers along one side of the town, or along a street, may be cleared out and measured ; then the next chambers inwards are cleared, and the stuff all thrown into the first row of chambers ; thus gradually turning over every scrap of rubbish without destroying a single wall, and leaving the place as well protected by its coat of *débris* as it was before the work.

The most fatal difficulty in the way of reaching what is wanted is when an early site has been occupied in later times. A city may have been of the greatest importance, and we may be certain that beneath our feet are priceless monuments ; but if there are twenty or thirty feet of later rubbish over it all, the things might almost as well be in the centre of the earth. Tanis was the Hyksos capital, but it would cost tens of thousands of pounds to lay bare the Hyksos level. The town of the twelfth dynasty at Illahun, on the contrary, yielded a harvest of small objects and papyri, revealing all the products and habits of that remote time, at a cost of two or three hundred pounds; simply because it was unencumbered. The temple of Ephesos cost sixteen thousand pounds, and almost a life's work, to discover it, owing to its depth under the surface. Naukratis and Defenneh, on the contrary, gave us the remains of the archaic Greeks, merely for the picking up and a little grubbing, both together not costing a thousand. It is plain enough that the main consideration is an accessible site.

An excellent rule in excavating is never to dig anywhere without some definite aim. Form at least some expectation of what may be found; and so soon as the general clue to the arrangement is known, have clearly in the mind what you expect to find, and what is the purpose of every separate man's work. One may be following the outside of a fortification, another trenching across it to find its thickness, another sinking a pit inside it to find the depth of the soil, another clearing a room, or trenching to find the limits of the town, or removing a rubbish deposit layer by layer. Unless just beginning work on a very featureless site, the aimless trenching or pitting is merely an excuse for a lazy mind. Far better have some theory or working hypothesis, and labour to prove it to be either right or wrong, than simply remain in expectancy. When you know what to look for, the most trivial indications, which otherwise would seem to be nothing, become of great importance and attract the eye. And the workmen should be encouraged to know what to expect beneath the surface, as it prevents their destroying the evidences. A vertical junction a few inches high, clean sand on one side and earth on the other, will lead to tracing the whole plan of a destroyed temple; a little patch of sand in the ground will produce a foundation deposit to your hands, and give the age of a building which has vanished; a slightly darker soil in a trench will show you the wall of a town which you are seeking; some bricks laid with mud instead of sand in a pyramid will point the way to the sepulchre. A beginner is vastly disappointed that some great prize does not turn up after a week or two of work; while all the time he is probably not noticing or thinking about material for historical results that is lying before him all the time. Perhaps in some place nothing whatever may be found that would be worth sixpence in the antiquity market; and yet the results from walls, and plans, and pottery, and measurements, may be what historians have been longing to know about for years before.

It need hardly be said that the greatest care is required in making certain as to exactly where things are found. Workmen should never be allowed to meddle with each other's lots of potsherds or little things; and any man mixing up things from elsewhere with his own finds should be dismissed. Men should be trained by questioning to report where they found objects, at what level and spot in their holes; and the best men may in this way be led up to astonishing intelligence, observing exactly how they find things, and replacing them as found to illustrate the matter.

M

In order to encourage the men to preserve all they find, and to prevent their being induced to secrete things of value, they should always be paid as a present the market price of such things at that place, and a trifle for any pottery or little scraps that may be wanted. To do this properly it is needful to know the local prices pretty closely, so as to ensure getting everything, and on the other hand not to induce men to foist things into the work from other places. Wages are paid by measure wherever possible, as it avoids the need of keeping the men up to the work, and is happier for both parties. Some day-work intermixed where measurement is impossible will often suffice.

It would be thought at first that nothing could be easier than to know a wall when you see it. Yet both in Egypt and Palestine the discrimination of mud-brick walls from the surrounding soil and rubbish in which they are buried, is one of the most tedious and perplexing tasks. To settle what is a wall and what is washed mud, and to find the limits and clear the face of the wall, is often a matter of half-an-hour's examination. The two opposite ways of working are by trenching sections through the wall, or by clearing the faces of it. The first is clumsy, but is needful sometimes, especially if the wall is much like the soil, and the workman cannot be trusted; as, if the face is cleared, the whole outside may be cut away without leaving any trace. The light on the surface is all-important, as any shadows or oblique lights mask the differences of the bricks; either all in sunshine, or better, all in shade, is needful to see the bricks. A distant general view will often show differences of tint in the courses, yellow, red, brown, grey, or black, which prove the mass to have been brickwork. The most decisive test is the difference at a vertical joint between bricks, as that cannot be simulated by natural beds of washed earth, as courses sometimes are. The lines of mud mortar are also different in colour to the bricks, and show out the courses. But yet all the question of joints is deceptive sometimes, owing to fallen bricks lying flat, and even fallen lumps of wall. In order to see the surface it must be fresh cut, or better, fresh broken by flaking it with picking at the face; by chopping successively back and back, each cut flakes away the mark of the previous blow, and so leaves a clean fractured surface all over. It must be remembered that bricks are often bent out of form by solid flow of the wall under great pressure, so that they may be distorted almost like a glacial deposit. In cleaning down the face of a wall it may often be traced by its hardness, but this is not a test to be left to workmen, or they may cut away at random; a very good plan is to let the man trench along a few inches outside of the face of the wall, and then cut down the remaining coat of rubbish oneself, to bare the face. Though pottery, stones, &c., often serve to show what is accumulated soil, yet they are found in brick sometimes, and must not be relied on entirely. The texture of the soil is important, as in accumulations all long bodies, bits of straw, &c., lie flat; whereas in brick they are mixed in all directions. Also washed-down earth almost always shows worm casts in it. Often a wall, if in low wet soil, will show out distinctly when the cut surface has dried, as cracks will form more readily along the joints. In many

cases, however, all of these tests hardly serve to
unravel the puzzle ; especially where there are successive walls superposed, and only a small height of any
one to examine. To trace out the position of ancient
walls is, however, one of the first requisites in such
work ; not only do we recover the plan of the town and
its buildings, but we are led thus to recognize what
may be the most important sites for special excavation.

One of the most difficult questions always is to know
what may be safely thrown away. Most trivial things
may be of value, as giving a clue to something else.
Generally it is better to keep some examples of everything. No matter how broken the potsherds may be,
keep one of each kind and form, replacing it by more
complete examples as the work goes on. Thus the
collection that is kept is always in process of weeding.
It need hardly be said that every subject should be
attended to ; the excavator's business is not to study
his own speciality only, but to collect as much material
as possible for the use of other students. To neglect
the subjects that interest him less is not only a waste of
his opportunities, but a waste of such archaeological
material as may never be equalled again. History,
inscriptions, tools, ornaments, pottery, technical works,
weights, sources of imported stones, ethnology, botany,
colours, and any other unexpected subject that may
turn up, must all have a due share of attention.
And keeping up the record of where everything has
been found, and all the information that will afterwards be needed, about the objects and the discoveries,
the measurements and details for publication, is a
serious part of the work.

However much it may be desired to preserve some things, they almost defy the excavator's care. It is a simple affair to get an antiquity safe out of the ground, but then begin its perils of destruction, and unless carefully attended to, it may slowly perish in a few days or weeks. The first great trouble is salt; it scales the face of stones, or makes them drop off in powder; it destroys the surface of pottery; it eats away metal. In all cases where salt exists it is imperative to soak the objects in two or three changes of water, for hours or days, according to the thickness. I have done this even with rotten wood, and with paper squeezes. Another source of trouble is the rotting of organic materials, wood, string, leather, cloth, &c. For all such things the best treatment is a bath of melted wax. But innumerable questions arise as work goes on, which can only be settled according to their circumstances: still, the soaking bath and the wax pot are the main preservatives.

The excavator should always be ready to take squeezes or photographs at once when required, and it is the best rule always to copy every inscription as soon as it is seen. If only an hour had been spent on the stele of Mesha, how much less should we have to regret! There is always the chance of accidents, and no risks should be run with inscribed materials. Even when the owner will not allow a copy to be made, the most needful points may be committed to memory, and written down as soon as possible, even under guise of making notes on other subjects. Another matter in which it is essential that an excavator

should be proficient, is surveying and levelling : in
order to understand a place and direct the work, in
order to preserve a record of what is done and make it
intelligible to others, a survey is always needed, and
generally levelling as well.

Lastly, what most persons never think of, a great
deal of time and attention is required for safely packing a collection. This part of the business generally
takes about a fifth of the time of the excavations ; and
much care and arrangement has to be bestowed on
the security of heavy stones, or pottery, or fragile
stucco, or glass, for a long journey of railways and
shipping. Packing with pads, with clothes, with
chopped straw, or with reeds, hay, or straw, is more
or less suitable in different instances. Finding things
is but sorry work if you cannot preserve them and
transport them safely. Most people think of excavating as a pleasing sort of holiday amusement ; just
walking about a place and seeing things found : but
it takes about as much care and management as any
other business, and needs perhaps more miscellaneous
information than most other affairs.

CHAPTER XIII.

THE FELLAH.

IT is always difficult to realise the state of mind of another person, even of one who is perhaps an equal in education, and who has been reared amid the same ideas and surroundings as one's own ; but it is impossible to really take the same standpoint as one of another race, another education, and another standard of duty and of morals. We cannot, therefore, see the world as a fellah sees it ; and I believe this the more readily because after living the most part of ten years among the fellahin, and being accused of having gone some way toward them, I yet feel the gulf between their nature and my own as impassable as ever. One measuring-line may perhaps give some slight idea of their position. The resemblances between Egypt of the present and mediaeval England are enough to help our feelings in the matter. There is the same prevalence of the power of the great man of the village ; the same rough-and-ready justice administered by him ; the same lack of intercommunication, the same suspicion of strangers : the absence of roads, and use of pack animals, is alike ; the lack of shops in all but large towns, and the great importance of the

weekly markets in each village, is similar again; and
the mental state of the people seems to be somewhat
akin to that of our ancestors.

The man who can read and write is the rare excep-
tion in the country; perhaps two per cent. of the
fellahin men can do so, but probably not one woman
in ten thousand. Of education there is but very little,
for the great majority of the people; in villages the
children of the fellah seldom go to school, and in
large towns the scholars are but a minority of the
boys, while the girls are nowhere. In accounts they
have some sharpness, but their reckoning would amuse

113. HOUSES IN THE DELTA, WITH RAIN-PROOF DOMES.

an infant scholar in England. I overheard some quick
lads, of about sixteen, anxiously discussing what a
man's wages were at £3 a month : they pretty soon
saw that it was £1, or 100 piastres, every ten days,
but how many piastres a day that was puzzled them
all. One fellow proposed eleven ; he was contradicted
by another who said twelve; then another tried $9\frac{1}{2}$;
and at last, as a great discovery, one sagely reminded
them all that ten tens made a hundred, and so a
hundred piastres in ten days *must* be ten piastres a
day. Egypt would almost satisfy Jack Cade.

The gross superstition, and the innumerable local

saints, remind us again of mediaeval times. Many—
perhaps most—of the people wear charms, written on
paper, and sewn up in leather; they are worn around
the neck, on the purse or pouch, or on the top of the
cap. Cattle are also sometimes protected by them.
It is common also for a man passing a saint's tomb to
repeat a prayer in a low mumble, even without stopping; while many go into the tomb-chamber to pray.
These saints are anybody who has died in an odour of
sanctity, probably within this century or the last—for
few, I imagine, have a perennial reputation. Some of
the great saints are commonly appealed to in the
slightest emergency, such as lifting a weight or climb-
ing an obstacle; and constant appeals are made to
Ya Said, ya Bedawi, ya Tantawi ('O Said, O
Bedawi, O man of Tantah') or *Ya sitteh Zenab* ('O
lady Zenab,' the wife of the prophet); while a Copt,
if his legs are stiff in rising from the ground, will call
out, *Ya adrah Mariam* ('O virgin Mary'). The
most absurd tales are readily believed, and there is
little or no discrimination or criticism applied to them.
At one village there lies a large number of rough
stones half hidden in the ground, scattered over
an acre or so; probably old remnants of building
material, brought a century or two ago from the hills.
A great festival of a local saint is held at the village
yearly, and an intelligent fellow gravely told me that
the saint had been murdered there with all his
followers, of whom a thousand were buried under each
of the stones. The total number, or the question of
burying a thousand men in a few square yards, did
not seem to matter. I have also heard the old tale

of the man who stole a sheep and ate it: when questioned, he denied the theft, whereat the sheep bleated in his stomach. A station-master, who had been educated in England, told me in English, in all sincerity, a tale about a Copt he knew, who got great treasures from a hall full of gold in an ancient mound. The door of the place only opened for five minutes once a week, on Friday noon, just when all true believers are at mosque; then the Copt went and took

114. HOUSES IN MIDDLE EGYPT.

all the gold he could carry, before the door shut. One day, tarrying, the door began to shut and wounded his heel before he could escape.

While naming the local festivals above, it may be noted that they generally take place around a tall pole fixed in some open space by the village. Some poles are stout masts thirty or forty feet high: around this central point is the celebration of the *molid* or birth-days of the village saint. Some *molids* are fairs for the whole district, lasting nine days or even more, and attended by performers, shows, jugglers, sweet-sellers, and as much riff-raff as any English fair.

Many visitors to Egypt see the dancing and howling derwishes, but few know of the common and less obtrusive orgies of the same kind in the villages. They are connected strictly with a devotional senti-ment : a man who has just joined in such excitement will tell you that it is 'good to see Allah' in that way—much like the fervid and maddening religious intoxication which yet finds a place in English civil-ization. These derwish parties are formed from a few men and boys—perhaps a dozen or twenty—who happen to live as neighbours : they are almost always held in moonlight, generally near full moon, a point which may connect them with some pre-Islamite moon-worship ; and though often without any cause but idleness, yet I have noticed them being held after a death in a village where they do not occur other-wise. A professed derwish often leads the party, but that is not essential. ' The people all stand in a circle, and begin repeating *Al-láh* with a very strong accent on the latter syllable ; bowing down the head and body at the former, and raising it at the latter. This is done all in unison, and slowly at first ; gradually the rate quickens, the accent is stronger, and becomes more of an explosive howl, sounding afar off like an engine ; the excitement is wilder, and hideously wild, until a horrid creeping comes over you as you listen, and you feel that in such a state there is no answering for what may be done. Incipient madness of the intoxication of excitement seems poured out upon

them all, when at last they break down from exhaustion;
or perhaps one or other, completely mad for the time,
rushes off into the desert, and is followed, for fear he
may injure himself. After a pause, some other phrase
is started, and the same round is gone through. After
about half an hour of this they separate with a great
sense of devotional virtue, and wearied with excitement.

Some curious observances are connected with acci-
dental deaths. Fires of straw are lighted one month
after the death, around the ground where the body

115. Houses in Upper Egypt.

has lain ; and where blood has been shed iron nails
are driven into the ground, and a mixture of lentils,
salt, &c., is poured out. These look like offerings to
appease spirits, and the fires seem as if to drive away
evil influences. Funeral offerings are still placed in
the tombs for the sustenance of the dead, just as they
were thousands of years ago.

The very hazy notions about all foreign places, and
the blankness of ignorance concerning surrounding
Nature, is a strong reminder of mediaeval times. To
say that the earth is round is flat heresy in Egypt ;

and even the *ulema* of Cairo—learned in all the wisdom of Islam—walked out of the government examination room to which they had been invited when a pupil was examined in geography. To listen to a description of a round world was too atrocious an insult to them. The dim ideas of Europe—some far-off heathenish land of infidels—and the questions as to how many Muslims there are in our towns and villages, show the peasant, even when intelligent, to be much on a level with the audience of Sir John Mandeville. It is no wonder that in such ignorance there is a mighty fanaticism. Islam is all in all to the fellah : the unbelievers he looks on as a miserable minority ; and it is only the unpleasant fact that they cannot be crushed at present that prevents his crushing them, and asserting the supremacy of Islam. A clever Arab once remarked to me concerning a department which was mismanaged by European direction, ' How much better it would be to have an Arab over it ! ' But on my asking where he could find a native whose corruption would not be far worse than the present rule, he could but reluctantly give in. This fanatical feeling of dislike to the Nusrani, or Nazarene, was the mainstay of Arabi's revolt ; and the very existence of such a feeling shows how dangerous it might become if fed on success. The children unintentionally reveal what is the tone and talk of the households in private ; they constantly greet the European with howls of *Ya Nus-rani* (' O Nazarene '), the full force of which title is felt when your donkey-boy urges on his beast by calling it, ' Son of a dog ! son of a pig! son of a Nazarene ! ' Any abuse will do to howl at the infidel, and I have been for months shouted at across every field as *Ya khawaga mafeles!* ('O bankrupt foreigner'), because I preferred walking to the slow jolt of a donkey. The fact that dozens of the villagers were depending on me for good pay all the time did not seem to weigh in the youthful mind, compared with the pleasure of finding a handy insult. This temper, if not held down, might easily rise in the arrogance of its ignorance to such a height as to need a much sharper lesson than it has ever received. That a massacre of the Coptic Christians was fully anticipated by them when Arabi drove out the foreigners, is a well-known matter of history, which should not be lightly forgotten.

This fanaticism is linked with an unreasoning ferocity of punishment. I have seen a coachman suddenly seize on a street-boy, and, for some word or gesture, lash him on the bare legs with the whip again and again with all his might. Even a particularly good-natured and pleasant native remarked with gusto how good it would be to take a certain family who were of thievish habits, and pour petroleum over them—from the old woman to the baby—and so burn them all up alive: he gloated over the throughness of the undertaking, while all the time he was cheating his own employer. It is a pity for their sakes that they do not believe in witchcraft, the whole village would so much enjoy the festivity of doing a ducking, in the fashion of our ancestors.

Akin to this fanaticism is the ruling view of everything as *kismet*, the allotted fate. Perhaps no abstraction is so deleterious to a character as this;

as a man always can thus shut his eyes to the consequences of his own actions, and refuse to learn by
experience. I never yet found a fellah who confessed
to doing wrong, or to being sorry for what he had
done. He may sometimes stand and look aghast
at the consequences of his own carelessness; but he
will do no more, and no less, if the damage is the
fault of someone else. He scarcely can, in fact, express
what one of ourselves would feel, as there is no word
for repentance in his vocabulary, except 'good'; nor
is there any word for sorrow, except 'angry' or
'annoyed.' The very sentiment of remorse is so
unknown that there are no means of expressing it
in any form. The constant way of appeasing an
injured party is for the offender to assure him emphatically that it is of no consequence (*ma'alesh*); and
the more often he thus asserts that he has not done
the other a wrong, the more he considers he clears
himself of it, until after sufficient of this lying he goes
away with a sense of virtue. If in consequence of
some very plain fault a man is punished by dismissal
or otherwise, expressly pointing out to him the causes
of his punishment, he will sullenly shrug his shoulders
and say to his companions, *Kismet*; it is fated he is
not to work. That any blame attaches to him for his
trouble seems not to be *dangable* into him by any means.
This lack of belief in consequences is also seen in the
extreme carelessness often shown. After a harvest, a
large quantity of grain had been stored in a room beside
a village, covered with the most inflammable of roofing
—durra straw: then, in order to toast some bread, a
blazing fire was lighted in the low room, and allowed to

flame up to the straw overhead. Of course it was soon all in flames, and the whole of a large proprietor's harvest was destroyed. Even when it was blazing, within a hundred feet of the canal, the only attempt to fetch water was by two or three women slowly filling their great pitchers and carrying them up on their heads as usual; no notion of a chain-gang ever seemed to occur to them. The same lack of any co-operation is seen when robbers are about. I asked why, when a house was attacked by thieves, the other villagers did not all come out and seize the men, being ten or twenty to one. The reply was, 'When anyone hears another house being robbed, he keeps as quiet as possible, and does nothing, for fear of attracting the thieves to his own house.'

This belief in *kismet*, and lack of co-operation, tells favourably in one way—the fellah is not revengeful. No matter whether he deserves what ill befalls him, or is an innocent sufferer, he never goes about for simple vengeance, but yields, and is ready to act as if no grudge or ill-feeling rested in his mind. What might be the case in an affront to their religion or family I would not say; but in all minor matters the fellah may be dealt with regardless of an idea of revenge.

The cardinal principle to remember in dealing with Egyptians is that they have no forbearance, and know no middle course. The notion of means exactly meeting an end, is outside of the fellah's sense. If he is careless about a danger, he is so careless in many cases as to be killed; if he thinks about it, he is so afraid that he will not face it at all. If he has to make anything secure, no amount of surplus security seems too great. If he knows that you have power, h e cannot be too submissive, and insists on kissing your hand, or at the least so honouring the aroma of it where it has touched his own. But if he has power himself, he gets all he can out of it ; and the grasping and overbearing nature of the village shekh is too generally well known to those under him. Nothing seems to have astonished and disgusted Stanley more than the scheming of the Egyptian soldiers, whom he expected to follow him, in retreating. Yet the whole affair was characteristically Egyptian : fleeing from the Mahdists ; only too glad to find anyone so foolish in their eyes as to be troubled about them ; and then clumsily plotting—without any regard to time—for making the best profit they could out of the affair, by seizing whatever seemed to have come.into their power. It would have been nothing to them to make away with people who were so indiscreet as to put ammunition within their grasp. The scheme seems to be the natural course of things to anyone who has watched the ways of Egypt. Peremptory orders are understood ; and the more peremptorily they are enforced the more cheerfully they are obeyed, though roughness or harshness is seldom necessary : but if you do not rule, you must submit to be ruled. And the fellah has a positive dislike to having a choice of action left to him. In matters indifferent to me, I often tell them to do what they please ; and that generally ends in their helplessly doing nothing, especially if they need to co-operate. At last, seeing their trouble, I give a precise order, and every one at once obeys it with thankfulness.

N

From this it follows that the fellah is one of the most easily managed people in the world. When once he knows who is master, there is little or no trouble. And if you can pick and choose your men, and keep them well in hand, instantly dismissing any who may disobey, it would be impossible to find a more cheerful, pleasant, well-disposed, and kindly set of fellows. The only danger is that they may perceive too much of your confidence in them. All the best men I have had have gone lamentably to the bad when they found that they were at all trusted. The temptation of having any credit of character is too great for them; they hasten to commute it for instant advantage, as soon as they see that there is anything to be made of it. The goose that lays golden eggs has a short and perilous life in Egypt.

That there is scarcely any sense of honour as to truthfulness need hardly be remarked. The idea of truth for its own sake does not weigh appreciably against either present advantage or serving the interest of another. The most respectable fellahin I have known would lie readily and unlimitedly, if they thought it beneficial. One very good fellow came to tell me one day what he had heard, prefacing it by saying how he had not two minutes before obtained the information by solemnly promising never to tell me about it. That he avowed the most un-blushing and deliberate lying never seemed to occur to his mind as anything noticeable, but rather a virtuous attention to my interests. Another superior fellow lost some letters, which were entrusted to him to post: when he came back he mentioned the loss, without any regret, and immediately went on to praise himself for the great virtue he had shown in acknowledging it, and the elevation of his moral standpoint above the sinners around him. It was, perhaps, a triumph of candour for an Egyptian.

From all that we have just noticed it will be plain that Egypt is a land of bribery. Every person who wants anything pays for it; time, attention, favour, facilities, screening, and escaping, all have their price. And it is the length of this price that is the deterrent from crime, and the dread of those who get into trouble over any affair. I reported a case of a villager throwing a dead buffalo into the canal. A policeman visited the shekh to enquire; a sovereign changed hands, and he returned stating that it was all a mistake, and that no dead buffalo ever existed there. But a few weeks later another policeman in search of prey rode round; and, finding a dead dog, pocketed a dollar for his acuteness. And the policeman is the fellah in trousers, armed, and in authority. A good false accusation will sometimes do, and is even occasionally worked on a wholesale scale for small bribes. Briefly, it may be stated that the working of petty jurisdiction is, that the law lays down what are offences, and attaches certain penalties to them; these penalties, then, roughly are the maximum limits to which the police can reward themselves by the discovery of such offences. The system works all right in the long run, as well as any system could in so corrupt a country: it is part payment by results to the police, with a minimum daily wage secured to them, and the pickings in proportion to their acuteness. Of course all this is profanity to the

ears of High Officials, who never have a chance of
hearing the quiet doings in the villages. The European
dignitaries, and many of the natives also, duly and
diligently administer justice when an affair comes to
their ears; but the little minor assaults and thefts
and squabbles are adjusted on a rougher and readier
system, which had better be left alone if it cannot be
improved away altogether.

The barrier which exists between the fellah and
the European official is almost insurmountable. Not
many officials visit the country districts at all; when
they do they stop at the shekhs' houses, and are always
attended by servants, before whom no man would
speak if he could avoid it, as they would talk about
him to the natives in the offices. Then the fellah is
timid, dreads men who go about on prancing horses,
and wear riding-boots and spurs—all that means
police and terrorism to him. Unless therefore there
is something very seriously amiss, the fellah in general
will not fly to the European official, on the rare
occasion when he sees him in the distance, and get
himself into the fire by trying to put someone else
into the frying-pan. If anyone wanted to learn what
was going on, and what was the state of affairs, let
him go on foot occasionally and tramp through some
villages, chat to the people by the way, avoid the
shekhs like poison; and, while not at all disguising
who he was in conversation, move about in as different
a manner to the ordinary official as he possibly can.
Some wiseacres have even said, 'Well, let them petition
if there is anything amiss.' Petition, indeed! from
people who cannot write, and have no knowledge

in general of who is the proper official to appeal to. or where he is! If they go to one of the clerks at the wayside—where they sit about the office doors,—he will at once inform the natives in the very office which may be in fault : if they go to the village scribe, he is generally a right-hand man of the shekh, who may be the very defendant in question. No! European administration, except in important or flagrant cases, scarcely touches the life of the fellah directly.

When I first met the fellah, I had always impressed upon me by an old Arab that no one ever did any-thing rightly unless they were heartily afraid ; and though this may be a harsh way to state it, the fact is true at bottom. There is no need to terrorise or to bully, and with most Egyptians perfect suavity is the best course ; but if a man transgresses in any way he must be met by sternness, and emphatically put into his right place. One of the most effective of minor rebukes is to raise a laugh at the transgressor among the bystanders : to make a man's doings ridiculous to his neighbours crushes him more than any expos-tulations. The fellah has a good sense of the ludi-crous, though he very seldom originates a joke. I have known little comparisons or nicknames that I have given, taken up all round by the people with a relish, and be repeated sometimes for days afterwards. Nothing smoothes matters more than getting them into a cheerful mood ; and I have often watched the faces when a discussion or difference has occurred, and by just throwing in a remark when a passing smile appeared, to bring it out into a laugh, the scale has been turned and business settled. The native in general squabbles over a difference with his fellows, shouts, and insists, shows fight, seizes the garments of his opponent, and threatens to tear them ; all for, per- haps, a pennyworth of advantage one way or other. They think equally that persistent worrying will wear out the determination of the European ; and, until they learn by long experience, they will try that method.   I have known a shekh stand facing me for over half an hour persisting that I should employ certain men to work for me ; and, though my refusals increased in strength, it was not until he was wearied out that he ceased : it is a simple battle of endurance in such cases.   He knew that his position would prevent direct personal ejection by force, and he accordingly used up that forbearance as so much leverage for his request.

Two principles of the fellah nature which Europeans cannot realise at first are that they cannot exercise forbearance, as we have noticed ; and secondly, that they cannot stand long-continued temptation.   Resi- dents sometimes say that the native is incurably bad ; that he may serve you for years, and rob you at the end.   But such cases are really the fault of the em- ployer, who has no more right to tempt people to rob him than to tempt them to murder him.   To reconcile such a view of the fellah with the astonishing honesty and particularity that I have often found, may seem difficult.   But time is the source of the difference. A man who will at once correct his accounts against himself, or bring you some trifle that you have over- looked or forgotten, will be quite incapable of even far less honesty, if the temptation is before him for months. Their impulses are generally sound and honest; but if they begin to look on anything as being in their hands, they drift easily into regarding it as their own. It is only a more rapid application of what may be seen in England regarding long trusts, charities, tenant-right, &c. The straightforward honesty that I have found on most occasions when an immediate temptation was before the fellah, has surprised me, and makes it needful to remember that this must not be strained and tried by continual temptation, the exposure to which will almost certainly spoil the character, and oblige one to cast aside a man who might otherwise have been useful and honest. Knowing this, I regard these failings of the fellah as lying quite as much at his employer's door as at his own.

One of the pleasantest points of the Egyptian character is the genuine and unfeigned hospitality so often met with. If in walking through a village I happen to pass the shekh sitting at his door, he will usually press the stranger to come in and have coffee, and hardly take a refusal. When pitching tent for the night, it is well to avoid coming under the shekh's notice, or probably he will insist on your stopping in his house : and in the larger towns the shekhs have sometimes excellent guest-chambers, with European furniture. This is hospitality for which no return is expected, or would be accepted. Even with poor people it is the custom for them to press one to stay, and to have coffee or food with them. An Egyptian travelling in England would think it very brutal that neither the squire nor any of the inhabitants of a village should press him to stay for a meal or for the night with them : he would set us down as shamelessly mercenary, and without any sense of propriety or generosity.

It is certain that the perceptions of an Egyptian are far less keen than ours. Their feeling of pain is hardly comparable with our own : with bad injuries, such as torn or crushed fingers, they do not seem at all distressed ; and a boy said to me that it was no wonder I healed quickly, as I did not disturb a wound, ' whereas an Arab would pull a cut open to look at it inside.' With pain, so with the senses in health. They cannot distinguish one person from another by the footstep ; they do not easily distinguish a voice ; they seldom respond or seem to perceive any words when called from a distance, unless the attention is aroused by loudly calling the person's name ; they never notice slight or distant sounds, and seem to suppose that you will never perceive a whisper from one to another. That the sense of smell is not much developed is only too evident from the fearfully filthy condition of the village surroundings, which are sometimes poisonous to an European.

Unfortunately the result of education is rather to spoil than to develop natural ability. Of the very few peasants I have met with who had been taught to write, two were fools in other matters, all common sense and ability appearing to have been crushed out of them. Nor is this at all surprising, when we know that the cardinal part of Muslim education is the learning of the pointless prolixities of the Koran by heart, as a pure matter of rote, without the use of the reason or intellect. To burden a child's mind with such a fearful task is enough to ruin it, if not strong. It is a sad sight to see the whole of the coming intellects of a town rocking themselves to and fro while they gabble through *sura* after *sura* of the Koran in a gusty sing-song voice without pause or point ; and then to reflect that this is the end and aim of nearly all their education. The native Coptic schools are the only encouraging sight of indigenous training ; and the ability shown by some of their boys is astonishing.

What then can we look forward to ·as the hope of improvement of such a people ? In the first place, a strong and just government, with a sufficient amount of an incorruptible European element to crush out bribery and ensure justice ; this, in a couple of generations, would go far to alter the national character. To trust one's money to the care of the government at the post-office, is the idea which astounds a fellah more than anything else he can learn of England. An education in which the Koran is but incidental, and not a crushing load on the memory, is another necessity. A spread of some sanitary ideas, and a cheap supply of some staple medicines for the commonest ailments, would be a great step : the utter ignorance and lack of all common sense in such matters is appalling. Probably improved dwellings, on some large estates, would be the most powerful means for changing their notions ; only such must not be Europeanised, but thoroughly native houses reasonably arranged as to ventilation, dryness, and disposal of all refuse ; thus they might lead to imitation; and a small premium on well-built houses would push the subject. The labour of devoted missionaries has already done a good deal in the way of education, and in the circulation of Christian literature; but hitherto hardly more than the foundation for further work in this direction has been laid. That English influence has a vast field for philanthropic enterprise in this six millions of people is obvious; but the best intentions may be too easily nullified by ignorance of the conditions of the case, and by the incapacity and resistance of the average native official, by whom it is useless to expect any serious change or solid advance to be carried out.

CHAPTER XIV.

THE ACTIVE TRIPPER IN EGYPT.

So much is Egypt the resort of the invalid, that the guide-books seem all infected with invalidism; and to read their directions it might be supposed that no Englishman could walk a mile or more without an attendant of some kind. In reality, Egypt is one of the most delightful countries for a walking tour, as regards circumstances. For three months from the middle of November there will never be a day too warm for active exercise; there will be hardly any rain above Cairo, nor as much in the Delta as during the summer in any European country. There is the same safety as in England or France: in very lonely places, as upon the desert, an occasional robbery may be committed, but I have never been molested by either fellahin or Bedawin. Of course, the native language is as much needed as in any foreign country; but a sufficient amount of colloquial Arabic can be learned in a few weeks. Three friends of mine have come out with only what could be briefly learned in England, and each has been able in a week or two to make his way sufficiently. Learn first of all what you want in Baedecker's vocabulary; refer to

Murray, or better, to a dictionary, for any further words you want; and absorb the addenda of very common words which come at the end of this chapter; then a week or two in Cairo, talking to the natives as much as possible, would quite suffice to float the active tripper. The main trouble is to catch what is said to you; and for this there is no better practice than listening to short sentences heard in the streets, and analysing them.

Many would-be trippers think of Egypt as so vastly expensive that they dare not attempt it. I will therefore be explicit as to means as well as ways. The P. & O., Orient, &c., are a needless cost. If a long voyage is no objection, Moss's line from Liverpool to Alexandria will provide all sufficient comfort, for £14, or £24 return ticket; this is a favourite way of despatching the families of English officials, to save the trouble and cost of the Overland route. For quickness and cheapness the Messageries from Marseilles to Alexandria is best; the second class is excellent, as good as the first on some lines; cost about £14, from London in six days. But all except hand baggage should be sent to Alexandria by long sea route. From experience I can say that for all expenses from London for three or four months and back again, from £50 to £100 will suffice, according to the amount of travelling in Egypt, &c., including food and wages.

The great difference between Egypt and more civilized countries is the lack of inns. Alexandria and Cairo abound with hotels, and there are two or three at Luxor. Regular inns are to be found at most of the main towns in the Delta, and at Assuan, Assiut, Medinet el Fayum, and other large places, though mostly of a rough kind. Below these there are the Greek wine-shops in most towns, where some sort of shelter can be had. The country station-masters are often very obliging, and will allow a traveller to sleep in the waiting-room ; and—in the Delta at least— the village shekhs are very hospitable, and generally have a good guest-room, sometimes with European furniture. Some good pocket-knives, silver spoons, and such articles, should be taken for presents, if this accommodation is needed. Also, if going to places where rock tombs abound, excellent quarters can be had in them ; no dwelling is so warm at night and so cool in the day. But for any extended journey it is best to take a small tent, if not travelling by boat. Convenient little tents, seven feet square, with two poles, weighing altogether only about 30 lbs., can be had in Cairo for about twenty-five shillings : such an one can be pitched or packed in a few minutes, and goes on a donkey with all the other baggage.

Some servant is needful to look after the things when one is absent ; a grown-up donkey-boy will be useful, if the traveller does not speak Arabic easily, as he will have a smattering of English ; but he will be perhaps a doubtful character, and will want about 3 francs a day. Far the best is to get an un-sophisticated fellah from some village ; he will be more trusty, and will be glad of 1 or 1½ francs a day without food. If there was no other means convenient for finding a man, I should go to some country station, and ask the station-master or post-master to recommend some fellah whom they knew ; there would thus be a hold upon him ; and an advance of wages could be left with his guarantor, to satisfy him of one's good faith in the bargain. For going about away from the railway or Nile steamers, a donkey must be hired for the baggage ; there is no difficulty in getting one anywhere, and with the boy or man 2½ francs a day is plenty in the country, though 3 or 4 francs is the Cairo rate. If by any chance one is wanted for riding, remember that though there are native saddles, there are no stirrups in the villages.

As to food, if constantly moving about, not much can be taken in the way of stores. But fowls (4–5 piastres), eggs (twelve to twenty-four a piastre), rice and lentils can be bought anywhere. Bread is not always eatable, as some villages only make dirty little pats of maize ; but good (though heavy) flap bread is made at nearly all towns and most villages (four to eight flaps a piastre), and a day's supply in advance should be carried. If staying for some weeks at one place, or going in a boat, it is best to order out from England assorted boxes of stores, each box to contain all that is wanted for three weeks or a month ; tinned tongues, soups, salmon, jams, cocoa, tea, biscuits, &c. Otherwise some tinned goods (sardines, peas, &c.) can be got in most large towns ; and some canisters should be taken for sugar, salt, pepper, tea, and coffee ; the latter can be made in the cup as wanted. The essential articles of canteen are :— Petroleum stove ('Hero' size is most useful), with saucepan, kettle, and frying-pan, and a tin can with cork to carry petroleum (*gaz*, Arabic), as the stove must be emptied when travelling. *Gaz* can be bought in any large village, and if constantly moving, the kettle and frying-pan are not needful: the stove may be bought in Cairo, but perhaps not the best size. Cups, plates, spoons, forks, candles, matches, dusters, and galvanised pail can be got in any large town. For sleeping, a mattress is a mistake, as the same weight of blankets are as soft, more easily aired and packed, and can be used for warmth if needful. Take six blankets, laid one on the other and then folded over down the middle, and there are twelve thicknesses, of which three or four will serve for warmth above, and eight or nine for softness below, and the wind cannot get in on the turned-over side. To pack these, roll them tightly, with the crockery in the midst, and lash round with two cords; then wrap in a sheet of oiled cloth, large enough to spread between the blankets and the ground when sleeping, and rope up the bundle. All this may be bought in Cairo.

For medicines not much is needful; but in case of emergencies take sulphate of zinc (1 per cent. solution) for the eyes; quinine (5–10 grs. for fever, ½ p. c. sol. alone, or mixed with the previous, for eyes); carbolic acid (1 to 3 of oil for scrapes and cuts, &c.), and any special remedies needed. In general, diet is the main matter; aperients are needless with plenty of native bread and cooked tomatoes; and, on the other hand, if necessary, live on rice (very well boiled with a large amount of water), and avoid fat and sugar. The less clothing is used by day, and the more at night, the better ; the clear nights are usually down to freezing in the winter, even far up the Nile, while the day may be 70° to 80°. The main matter is to avoid being out at sunset ; or at least keep moving then, and avoid any chill, as fever is generally caught at that time. All drinking water should be boiled thoroughly ; excepting perhaps when taken from the middle of the Nile, and not just below a town.

For a trip up the Nile the most thorough way is to take a small native boat, with a cabin on it, entirely to yourself, or with only a like-minded companion. Such a boat can generally be found at the main towns, Cairo, Minia, Assiut, &c. ; when more pretentious, with several cabins, it ranks as a *dahabyieh*. The boat should be hired with a written English, French, or Italian agreement in duplicate, some European shop-keeper known to the boatman serving as his trans-lator, to assure him of the terms. The actual terms of a boat I hired at Minia were 'A. B. agrees to hire a boat with cabin from C. D., with a reis, two sailors, and boy, at ten francs per day. Ten days' hire guaranteed ; after that by the day. To be discharged anywhere below the first cataract (Assuan) without any return pay. No food provided. Payments to be made as demanded, taking receipts.' If they dawdle, and it is needful to push on quicker, a promise, of say 50 francs on reaching the terminus by a certain day, less 5 francs a day for all time after that, will be effectual. Always stay for the night above a town or village, for the sake of cleaner water.

If only the principal places are to be visited, the

postal steamer will suffice, taking tent, blankets, &c., to stay where desired. From Assiut to Assuan costs £5, without food; the cabins holding two or four, well fitted; and if all places are taken it is quite practicable to go on deck, sleeping in blankets (only 85 piastres). Passage can be taken between any two stations at proportional rates. When pitching tents, always stay by a village, and the shekh is responsible for your safety; look out for one of the little huts in which the village guards stay at night, and pitch ten or twenty yards in front of it; thus the guards will not come and sleep by the tent, for if they do their incessant talking or snoring will prevent any sound sleep. At Thebes the best camping ground is in the Ramesseum (the guards' head-quarters) and under a tree by the pylon of Horemheb; and at Assuan in the bay above the town.

There is no need to carry much money about, as the post-offices serve for banks; and the regular bankers and agents generally charge (by exchange, &c.) nearly or quite the 1 per cent. of the post. Postal money orders should be taken in England for £10 each, one or more as probably required, on each of the main towns visited. The best address for receiving the actual Egyptian orders (for English forms are useless) is Poste Restante, Alexandria, as any enquiries about them should be made there. The money is paid in English gold at the offices. All accounts are, however, paid in piastres, at 97½ to the sovereign.

In case of taking luggage about by train or steamer, remember that nothing goes free except what is carried.

O

All heavy things must be weighed, paid for, and a receipt obtained before the train leaves ; and baggage is only given up in exchange for the receipt (=*bolicy* Arab.). Exactly the same must be done for goods, which are usually despatched within twelve hours by goods train, at half the rate of passenger train. There is no delivery of goods ; everything must be claimed with the *bolicy* and fetched away. Carts cost about 1 to 2 francs the hour, and a bargain should be made with the driver for the whole business. If passenger luggage is left at stations the charge is heavy (3 p. each day or part for each parcel), but the station cleaner will look after things for a few hours. Goods are charged 1 p. per parcel per day at Cairo and Alexandria, but Sundays and 24 hours after arrival, free. At country stations the charges are next to nothing, and things may be sent by goods train and left for a week or two if necessary. Receipts are always given for every legal charge, however trifling ; but see that the amount asked for is what is written.

The above details are of course only supplementary to the usual guide-book information. But there is no real difficulty likely to be met with in roughing it thus ; and in case of emergencies the station-masters or post-masters can be appealed to, as they all understand English or French. Many of them have been in Europe, and I may say that I have received much kindness and friendliness from these excellent officials, who are largely Coptic Christians. They are above the common greed for petty bakhshish ; though of course kindness may be recognized by a book, photographs, or other presents, as to a European official. In most bargains for services, as with donkey-boys, camel-men, boats, guides, &c., it should be remembered that 5 to 10 per cent. extra is expected as bakhshish in a lump at the end, subject to good behaviour ; and this gives an excellent hold on the people.

ADDENDA TO BAEDECKER'S
VOCABULARY

—♦—

Station, *mahatta*; ticket, *tezkereh*, *warak*, *bilieto*; 1st class, *brimo*; 2nd class, *secondo*; (does) this go to Cairo? *deh raih al Masr*? train, *kattr*; engine, *wabur*; carriage, *arabiyeh*; goods, *buda'a*; goods train, *kattr el buda'a*; baggage-receipt, *bolicy* (pronounced *bolīse*); storage charge, *ardiyeh*. I (will) beat the telegraph (=I will telegraph), *ana adrob et telegraphia*; the wires, *es silk*.

(The dots in the following words separate the elements, which are here translated literally.)

Show·me the snake, *warri·ni el hanesh*. Not showed·I to·him the fowl, *ma warr·et l.u·sh el farkha* (*sh* like French *pas*, untranslated). Not·thou·leave·it, *ma·t·khalli·u·sh*. He opened·it, *Huweh fatah·u*. Thou earnest from where? *Ente git min ayn*. From the desert (hill or plain), *min el gebel*. Thou goest where? *Ente raih fen*. Northwards, *bahri*. The engine it·leaves when? *el wabur ye·safir emta*? at·the sunset, *fi·l maghreb*. Atest·thou five pounds in·the four·months, pound·and·quarter for the month, *kal·t khamast ertal fi·l arbat·usher, rotl·u·rub bi·sh shahr* (accent strongly as marked). Two cubits length (pair cubits) for two piastres (dual), *gozet ídra bi kirshēn*. Finished, *khalás*. I am very tired (I bad·ed entirely), *ana battal·t khálas*. Finished entirely, *Khalás khálas*. (It) was cold very in·the·morning before the sun(rise), *kan bard kowi fi·'s subh kabl esh shems*. The peasants (are) foolish like cattle, *el fellahin magnun zeyeh behaim*. A lucky day for you (literally, day·thy, milk) *neharak leben*. By life (of) the prophet, *wa hayt en nebi*. By life (of) father·thy, *wa hayt abu·k*. Bless me! (oh health·my) *ya salam·i* (really a title of the Deity).

Village night guard, *ghafir*, pl. *ghofera*.

INDEX

(Including a reference to each Illustration.)

———+———

THE END.

www.ingramcontent.com/pod-product-compliance
Lightning Source LLC
Chambersburg PA
CBHW040406110426
42812CB00011B/2464